MR. CHARMING (NOT)

ALPHALICIOUS BILLIONAIRES BOSS

LINDSEY HART

COPYRIGHT

All characters in this book have no existence outside the imagination of the author and have no relation whatsoever to anyone bearing the same name or names. They are not even distantly inspired by any individual known to the author, and all the incidents are pure invention. No part of this publication may be reproduced or transmitted in any form or by any means, mechanical or electronic, including photocopying or recording, or by any information storage and retrieval system, or transmitted by email without permission in writing from the publisher. While all attempts and efforts have been made to verify the information held within this publication, neither the author nor the publisher assumes any responsibility for errors, omissions, or opposing interpretations of the content herein. The book is for entertainment purposes only. The views expressed are those of the author alone and should not be taken as expert instruction or commands.

Edits by Charmaine Tan.
Cover by Cosmic Letterz.
You can contact the author, Lindsey Hart at:
team@lindseyhartromance.com

© Passion House Publishing Ltd 2021
All rights reserved.

BOOK DESCRIPTION

You know that dream you have about a Charming Prince sweeping you right off your feet with a kiss?

Well, that happened.
Except I'm the one who smacked that kiss right on Mr. Charming,
Without his permission.
Oh, and I also found out right after that he is actually my new boss.
And the world's most notorious playboy.

Way to go, Emily.
Time to get fired.
How much more worst can my life go at this point?
Oh, yes.
Maybe finding myself splashed on first page of all tabloids as the new Bosshole's playgirl.
But what probably takes the cake is ending up being blackmailed by the prick himself.

He needs me as his fake girlfriend... and he is counting in months, not days!
Because you know he needs time to get rid of his infamous A-Hole reputation for some reason.
Like that was ever going to be possible.

The sensible thing would be to keep away from him,
Not let his kisses mess with my head,
Keep my bloody hands to myself!
And oh yeah, maybe NOT fall in love with him.
Especially when I am hiding big stuff from him.

1

EMILY

I warned the bastard.

He fully knew what would happen to his stuff if he didn't come and get it. When I said I'd light it on fire, I truly meant it.

Three days ago, I joined the ranks of clichéd women all over the planet. The ranks of the cheated on, poor women who have a rock on their finger and the vague promise of happily ever after on the horizon and still come home to find their fiancé tupping another woman on the kitchen table.

Yes, that's right. *Tupping.* I actually have two degrees. One in English—in which I majored in classical lit and minored in theatre, because duh, they're an excellent fit together—and a second in business since the former didn't exactly pay the bills. And yes! Even with my two degrees, I'm still calling it *tupping*.

I was actually in school for six years, and thanks to my business degree, I currently have a job. I work for a company whose focus is ethical and sustainable fashion. Well, you know, clothes made with bamboo and hemp that are super soft, stylish, and planet-friendly. That's the company. My parents just can't figure out how I ended up here in the fashion world. Sometimes, I even amaze myself. I suppose that even though a person can't draw or sew, they can still work here as a manager, which I do. I worked my way up the ranks for the past five years to get to where I am.

Anyway, back to the tupper...I suppose he once had a name before he became dead to me. Byron the butthole. That's his name. Byron the bastard. Byron the burner of souls and destroyer of hope. Byron the bozo. He has quite the alliterative name.

And currently, at this very moment, Byron, the biggest butthole bastard in all of the land of burned souls and destroyed hopes, is standing outside my workplace. He's blowing up my phone with all sorts of sappy nonsense, but the long and short is that he wants me back. He says he's so very, very sorry and that he'll never stick his very um—well—inadequately sized fire poker into someone else's fireplace again. According to him, he's desperate to win back my trust. Blah, blah, bullshit, blah, bullshit, and even more bullshit.

Any other day, I'd march out there and send him off with a few very choice words, all while keeping my cool because the freak out has happened, and what's done is done. I've since made peace with the fact that the last three years of my life were totally for nothing, relationship-wise, at least. I was having doubts about getting married anyway, so he really did me a favor there.

Although, he's not currently doing me a favor by loitering outside when this morning is a big morning for me as well as for the rest of the place. We were just bought out by a huge name in the fashion industry. Julie Louise

Mr. Charming (Not)

Paris—I doubt that's her real name—has been designing haute couture since the eighties, and her stuff is the kind of thing you see in magazines and red carpets. You know those dresses that cost like six figures a piece? That would be her. She has shops in all the big and fancy cities around the world.

And we all know why she bought us out.

For her son.

Her son is a bit of a tupper himself. Or whatever. I don't really know anything about him other than what the magazines say, but we all took an interest after we found out we were being bought out and that he was going to be our new CEO. In his case, I'd say he's likely going to be our Clueless Executive officer. He knows everything about partying, spending money, dating models and actresses, pissing his grandmom off, spending her money, causing scandals—the usual rich people things—and nothing about actually working in the industry.

That's what people say, and it's basically all I have to go on.

My phone dings again, and I realize I've drifted off into a happier place. Sort of, though not really. When did my life turn into an epic poo pile? Well, I guess that would be eight days ago when we found out about getting acquired by Julie Louise Paris. I didn't think a week was a long time, but I've since learned otherwise. With a heavy sigh, I turn my attention to more of the bullshit, bullshit, and extra bullshit texts.

Byron: Buttercup, please come out and let me talk to you. I'm so, so sorry. I don't know what I was thinking. Please. Give me another chance.

Byron: Pleeeeeease! You know I love you! You know I'd do anything for you!

Apparently, that doesn't include monogamy, but maybe Byron thought it was supposed to come after the wedding, and the before bits didn't count.

Byron: Babe, you know you're the only one in the world for me. You're my princess. You're the most important person in my whole universe. I made a mistake. Please don't punish me. We can talk. We can sort this out. I'll pay for counseling. I'll do anything!

I don't even consider typing anything nasty in response. That would be low, and I'm not stooping to his level, in that direction, or any other. I'm done with Byron. We were one of those couples who should have broken up instead of getting engaged, so it's better that he did something before we had to go to the lawyers and pay a bunch of money to undo something else.

Still, I really can't handle this right now. In an hour, I'm supposed to go into a meeting with the rest of the company to get introduced to our new CEO, so I'm trying to focus on that and get into work mode. I'm also scared the jerkus of a CEO is going to ruin our company. Ever since I heard the news, I've been sweating about losing my job. Honestly, we're all scared, and coming into work the past week hasn't exactly been fun.

Byron: Sugarplum! Love of my life! Juliet to my Romeo! Please, come down and talk to me!

Oh no. He did not just invoke the bard. He's gone too far now.

I push back from my desk and fly out of my office. With purpose, I stride down the hall on the ground floor, take a right so hard at the reception desk that I nearly slip and fall on the tile floor—which would probably ensure a broken hip even at the age of thirty-one—and push out the glass door, right out in the streets.

Mr. Charming (Not)

Byron is right there. He really wasn't kidding about being on the doorstep.

"No!" I hiss before he can say a word. I jam a finger in his direction. "Just, no! There is nothing to say. We are done. Over. I'm changing my number as of freaking tonight, and the locks were changed days ago. You were warned. Anything you didn't come to get that day after your little performance is going to get burned. I'm done. We're done—end of story. Please leave here and don't come back. Don't come to my house, and don't come anywhere near me. If you do, I'll call the police and file a restraining order. I don't want you in my life. I can't be any clearer than that."

"Jeez," Byron sulks. He's one of those overgrown man-child types. I mean, he's handsome if you like shaggy blonde hair and the surfer kind of look. He would do alright in California, but we live in freaking St. Louis, so the vibe is kind of tiresome, especially since he's pushing thirty-five. "Redheads really do have serious attitude problems."

"My hair is *dyed*, you freaking moron!" I'm finished with this conversation. I can't even shake my head at his stupidity. Sure, I have fire engine red hair. But yeah, like as if it's natural. Byron has known me for three years, and I just started dyeing it last year because I wanted a change. I'd never done something funky, but when I finally did, I loved the look and decided to roll with it.

"What did you do with my laptop?"

Great. I just knew this was going to spiral down into a muck pit of grasping and moaning about the shit he left behind. I knew it was never actually about me because Byron cared more about living with me for free and letting me support him than he ever did about me as an actual person.

"I burnt it."

"No!" Byron's eyes get impossibly large and nearly goggle straight out of his head. "You didn't!"

"I actually didn't, but I did say you had one day, and you told me you already had all the shit you wanted. I literally have written evidence. So, if you want your laptop back, go down the street a couple of blocks over and check with the homeless guy who sits in front of the mall. It really made his day when I dropped it in his lap."

"You bitch!" Byron growled.

"Mmmhmm."

"I want the ring back! It's mine!"

You are seriously a loathsome, shitsome ballbag. I don't let that out because, shit, I don't want to encourage Byron to stick around a second longer. "It was actually mine. Anyhow, it's also been donated to someone who needed it more than either of us. If you really want to buy it back, check the pawn shops around here. I'm sure that's where it ended up."

"You...you..."

"You know what? I'm done with this. You need to leave, or I'll go in and get security."

Byron's tanned face becomes a shade brighter than my hair, which is incredibly impressive given that my hair is an amazing shade of wonderful. It was professionally done by a very talented stylist who I always tip well because she works miracles. *Miracles*, people.

"You'll never find someone else," Byron fumes. "This is your last chance to come back to me. We all know nerds like you don't get many dates."

"Nerds like me?" I snort derisively.

Mr. Charming (Not)

I could go on about nerds like me supporting bums like him, but it would be a waste of good air, and I plan to spend my breath on something that matters, not on vile assholes with undersized weenuses. I just shake my head, catching a glimpse of something tall, dark, and manly a few steps behind me. I guess my pride is a little bit wounded because I do something irrational even though I *never* act impulsively. I'm a thinker, and I usually move carefully before I act.

"Actually, I've already moved on, thank you very much. I just needed a push in the right direction. I'm very, very happy." I bite out the bit about wishing him good luck with moving back to his mom's place.

I pivot at exactly the right moment—irrational, spur of the moment plan in place. The rational, normal Emily would never just step into a guy's path, grab him off the street, cup his solid jaw and corded neck, and tug his face down. The careful Emily would never lock lips with a stranger, hoping the guy's indignation could be staved or laughed off after Byron goes sputtering and storming away in the opposite direction.

I guess this is the reactional, pissed off, with something to prove Emily because I do all of those things. I'm not athletic, but somehow, the timing all works out, and my lips hit a pair of the softest, hottest, most delicious lips I've ever encountered. Stubble scratches my cheek and grazes my fingertips as heat floods through my body, and a frantic pulse flutters where my fingertips rest on a total stranger's perfect throat. At the taste of deep and mysterious masculinity, as well as when the scent of spicy cologne invades my nose, an overwhelming urge to moan overtakes me as my heart explodes into a frantic rhythm.

I nearly pull back, an explanation and one heck of an

apology at the ready, when the stranger tangles a strong hand in my hair, tugging gently so that my face tilts back and he can deepen the kiss.

The whole frantic pace of St. Louis freezes around me. The world stops, time ceases, and for a moment, I think I might be living one of those classic romances I love so much, except they don't usually end so happily because people back then didn't buy into the notion of that—the whole happily ever after. Regardless, I do know for a fact that this is THE BEST KISS I've ever had in my life.

Never, in all my thirty-one years on this earth, have I ever been kissed like this.

This puts all other kisses to shame.

When my poor ambushed stranger, who kisses like the devil coming straight from hell to claim my soul, releases me, he chuckles low in his throat. The rumble seers right through me like I just stuck my head in a cannon, and someone fired it. Minus the ball, because my head is the ball, I think.

I don't know, as my mind has blanked, and the whole world is spinning crazily. I realize I've just done something very, very stupid. And that's before my vision clears, everything comes into focus, and I realize the perfect stranger I just grabbed and basically tongued right in the middle of the street like a shameless strumpet is none other than Asher Paris. My new boss.

Holy blasted bleepers, what have I done?

2

ASHER

I know it's a bad sign when Granny calls me before six in the morning. In case I had any doubts about her displeasure and thought she was calling to wish me well in my new venture, she starts the conversation with a hoarse growl.

"Your mom was a spoiled brat, and so are you. You've both given me hell. I mean giving. As in, still doing it. Both of you."

I groan and roll over in bed. It's a king-size bed since I'm staying at a hotel. I haven't even started my house hunt yet. All of this—the new company, putting me in charge—all of it was my Granny's idea, and apparently, she's already regretting it.

"For once, I have no idea what I've done."

There's a sound on the other end of the phone. It sounds like someone choking on a grape followed with a fly being wrathfully swatted, but I know better. The choking is my grandma at a loss for words because of the inherent stupidity of that denial, and the *whack* is the sound of scandal. Okay, so it's actually the sound of a rolled-up magazine hitting a countertop or some other hard surface, but seriously. This time, I have no idea why she's mad at me.

"You! You made the front page again! Of four different magazines, and I can't even count the rags. You promised to take this seriously!" Granny screeches.

"What?" I gasp and nearly drop the phone, then nearly drop myself when I throw back the sheets and jump out of bed. My heel gets caught, and I do a hop skip and another hop across the room, nearly landing in the full hot tub in the corner of the room. It burbles and bubbles at me, hiccupping water in invitation. "What are you talking about?"

"I'm talking about you with your tongue down some girl's throat all of two seconds into your arrival there! You weren't even through the front door! She works there! Of all the people—of all the places—of all the *evil* things!" Granny roars out the word *evil* like she's got a pitchfork sharpened and ready for me and is about to hand out some serious medieval-style justice.

"Seriously. Okay." The hot tub continues to bubble at me gracefully. "Okay, I did it. I did kiss her. I...I mean, it happened, but I didn't instigate it. She was standing there, and she grabbed me and just...did it. She was having an argument with someone. I think she just wanted to prove a point."

"She proved it all right!" Granny calms down and sighs. I can imagine her face, still beautiful, her big green eyes sad and tired, her lips wavering because even when she's angry with me, she still loves me more than anything on this earth, which makes me feel like a golden pile of shit for upsetting her.

"Granny, I—"

Mr. Charming (Not)

"I warned you," she hisses, cutting me off. "One more scandal, and you're out! You've given me one heart attack after another your whole adult life. Sixteen! This started when you were sixteen. You're double that now. For the past decade and a half, you've shaved years off my life. *Years!*" That's also roared out like the very *devil* was here.

I can practically feel that pitchfork of hers coming straight for my tender buttocks. I know I need to calm my grandma down quickly because she's right. I did promise, but I'm also right. This one, for once, wasn't my fault as I just happened to be in the wrong place at the wrong time. Or the right place, rather, because I was supposed to be there. Only at the wrong time. Although, that kiss didn't feel so wrong. It was honestly quite delightful. I mean, no. I hated it. Every single second of it. How dare that stranger just grab me and do something so intimate? In my head, I say it in my deepest, lecturing professor-style voice, deeply salted with sarcasm.

"I mean it," I say, hoping my grandma can hear the sincerity in my voice. "I haven't dated anyone for the past six months. I was so absorbed in work that I didn't have time. When you offered me this company, a fresh start, all of that, I wanted it. I still do. I really was just there, and she really did just kiss me. I didn't realize there were photographers, or I wouldn't have enjoyed the surprise so much if I had known."

"Asher! Of course there were photographers! You've given the media every reason to follow you around over the years. You have money, you're young, you're attractive, you're exciting, and you're bad. You're everything they eat right up and sell so everyone else can devour it."

"That's a little bit harsh, especially before six in the morning."

"I'll give you six in the morning, you little shizzle snizzle!" she growls.

I wince. Granny might be barely more than five feet tall, but when she starts bringing the curses, watch out. She's every bit as dangerous as a raging grizzly disturbed from hibernation. I also recall she's in Paris, and yeah, it's not exactly before six in the morning there. Not that I know what time it is, but I know she doesn't care. She called me the second she found out about the kiss.

"Granny…I really am sorry. I had no idea, and I haven't broken my promise. It truly was an accident. She kissed me, and I have no idea why. She took off right after, and I didn't see her again. I…please don't get upset. You might seriously damage something."

"Yes," Granny grunts. "You."

"No!"

"That company is an ethical clothing line. It puts good into the world. I bought it for you because I thought it's what you needed!"

Now she's using her despairing tone on me—the one she's used ever since I was somewhere around, well, birth. For as long as I can remember, she's always told me I'd put her into an early grave. She uses that *I'm fragile, I'm fading, this last act of yours is going to be the straw that shoves me right into an earth hole, and it will be all your fault* tone every single time. I can still remember her doing it to me when I was five years old. I stole a cookie before dinner, and she gave me that grave look. As in the grave. Her grave.

Despite all the guilting, my grandma is the best person I know. She's a great lady in all aspects of the word, and she more than raised me because my mom wasn't exactly capable of doing it all the time. I mean, my mom tried. I love both of them—my mom, even with her faults, and my grandma for sticking it out and never giving up on either of us. I feel kind of sorry for disappointing her. Again. It really has been a trend, and she has every right to the anger and hurt she's feeling.

"It is what I need. I do want to do this. Really." I do want to make her proud of me, as corny as that sounds. "You know if it were something I'd done, I'd own it. I've always done that."

"Ha!" Granny scoffs. "That you have. Ever since you were a kid—or should I say, a brat—and liked to run around breaking things and cutting the dresses I was designing."

Ugh. The ruined dress. Granny always brings that up. And I mean *always*. It happened when I was six, and still, her heart is in tatters about it. I don't think she'll ever get over it. I just got too happy with a pair of scissors, okay? I put a few small cuts in a dress on a dress form in Granny's house when she was babysitting me one night, and I also cut about a foot off my hair. My mom also never forgave my grandma for my ruined lovely locks that she'd been growing out since I was born. It was a bad scene all around.

"If you're serious about this, you fix your own mess this time," Granny says, though it's with more patience. Like she actually might believe me.

I've never cried wolf. I have always owned the messes I've made—mess, life experience, mistake...kind of everything.

"One day, they'll just get tired of me."

Granny scoffs at that, and I can imagine her eyebrows shooting to her pink hairline. Yes, her hair is currently pink, and yes, she's also sixty-five years old. "The women or the tabloids?"

"Both."

"The tabloids will get tired of you when you're settled down with someone, committed and in a sappy romantic relationship with your soul claimed and devoted. You'll be doting, smitten, bitten, whatever. All of it. That's the only way they'd get tired of you."

"Are you…are you suggesting I make things right by paying someone to be my fake girlfriend?" The line goes dead silent, and for a second, I'm worried that this time, the early grave thing worked. "Granny?"

"I'm still here," she barks. "That's a ridiculous thing to say. Money can buy a lot of things, but it can't buy love. We both know that."

She's right. Unfortunately, we both do. My mom too.

The hot tub bubbles in front of my face, and I don't know why I'm still standing in front of it, breathing in the warm fumes. "It's not a terrible idea," I say, putting it out there again. "I could find her and make her agree to make it look like we know each other. Like we knew each other before that kiss but kept it quiet. That I came here, not just for the company, but for her."

I expect my grandma to keep up with the protests, but there's a strange sound on the other end, like a frog croaking thing. "It might work."

I'm stunned. It's early, and I guess my muscle control isn't the best first thing in the morning because my clenched fingers release. My phone goes into a freefall, hits the edge of the hot tub, bounces once, then flops and descends into the watery depths.

I stare at the phone, my mouth hanging open. The crazy part is that I can hear Granny yelling at me from under the water for a few seconds before it dies, and everything goes silent.

Shit shizzle. That's one of Granny's favorite expressions. She's not exactly a token grandma. And this seriously is my last chance before she does something drastic like takes out a pair of scissors and does some snipping.

Not on me, but on her will. With my name. You know, the good ol' cutting me out deal. She's never actually threatened to do it, but I can sense it coming. Because who in our multi-billion dollar company would want at its head a playboy interested only in partying. It does not matter how hard I've worked or will work. If the media continues to paint me in this limelight, then I'm done. No way will I be accepted as the next head.

Anyhow, I know one thing. Well, I know a lot of things, but for the moment, just one. I need to fix this, and by fix it, I mean find the red-headed goddess who brazenly locked lips with me earlier today and convince her to act like she's my secret love, my only love, the love of my life. My one and only. The sweet to my bitter and the syrup to my maple. The jam to my peanut butter? The dipping sauce to my fish sticks?

Holy buns and bologna. I'm in serious trouble here.

I've never been in love before. Not. Once. I wouldn't know the first thing about faking it.

And apparently, I now need a bag of rice for my phone.

At least there's one positive thing about accidentally kissing one of my employees. She should be easy enough to find. Maybe. I really, really hope so anyway.

3

EMILY

*H*oly crap, what is Julie Louise Paris doing on my doorstep at nine on a Sunday morning? What is she doing on my doorstep at all?

I know it's her. Even if the bright pink hair didn't give her away, her lovely floral blouse, white slacks, and designer shoes and handbag would. She looks like a walking fashion show. Tall, statuesque, and lovely, even in her older age. She looks less like someone's grandmother and far more like a businesswoman intent on squashing something. Or rather, someone. Namely *me*.

"Urg!" I squeak. I snap my mouth shut, and my hand trembles on the door. "Um..." Apparently, that's the extent of any intelligent conversation for the moment.

One of her eyebrows arches artfully, and those liquid green eyes of hers—the color of moss—stare right through me. "May I come in?"

"I...why?" I sound like a mouse who just got caught in a trap. Not a pretty picture. Neither is my old fluffy purple housecoat or the tatty t-shirt and shorts I have on underneath.

Mr. Charming (Not)

"You have to know why. You've seen the magazines, I'm sure."

"What?" I squeak, my mind racing to try and understand what she means. What magazines?

"Come now, dear. It happened on Friday, and it's been two days. You can play coy with everyone else, but you should know one thing about me. Shooting straight is the only way to talk to Julie Louise Paris."

Holy crap, did she just talk about herself in third person? I realize I'm in serious trouble here because I don't know anything about magazines, but I do know what happened on Friday. I know I fled the scene, called our receptionist from down the block to say I'd suddenly been overwhelmed by some kind of barfing sickness and that I wouldn't be in until Monday morning. I spent Friday afternoon and also all of Saturday hunkered down, wondering how the heck I was going to fix my current predicament. My kissdicament.

AssholeByrondickingsomeoneonmykitchentabledicament.

"There...there's magazines? What kind of magazines?"

"Gossip kinds. My grandson is quite famous with them, and they follow him around like flies on a stench. What I want to know is if you kissed him or if he kissed you."

"I...I...I..." I drop my gaze to the ground while my heart beats so hard that the knocking against my ribs causes terrible ripples to vibrate up into my throat and close it off. *Magazines? How could this get any worse?* "I...I...m-might have kissed him."

Julie Louise Paris huffs. "This isn't a conversation I want to have outside on your wonderful doorstep. Invite me in for coffee."

"I...uh...alright." I dart my eyes down the street like

we're doing something illegal here—a shady deal of some sort.

Julie Louise Paris walks through the door like a queen. Though I suppose she is—a queen of the fashion world. It's crazy to meet her in person. She doesn't seem real. It's like she sent a clone or robot AI to trick me or perhaps murder me and hide my body downstairs where no one will ever find it. A robot could dig through concrete, pour fresh concrete, and weave a rug to cover up the spot. I'm sure of it. I shouldn't underestimate the power of technology.

I don't know what's worse. Thinking about a Julie Louise Paris murderous robot or finding the real Julie Louise Paris in my house, all the way from some far-flung corner of the world, here to talk to me *inside my house* about her grandson.

I want to break down and start bemoaning out loud the deplorable decision I made, the terrible timing, and how it somehow ended up in trashy magazines, causing Julie Louise Paris to be here now to either murder, fire, or buy me. However, all I can do is curse Byron under my breath.

I curse again when I realize I've walked into the kitchen. I stare at the table as Julie Louise Paris walks over, the picture of Byron with that hussy flashing before my eyes again. "No!" I blurt frantically as she pulls out a chair. "Not there!"

She backs up a step and stares at the table like there's a viper hidden underneath. With my face flaming red, I switch on the coffee pot, which I had ready before the knock on my door, and quickly exit to the living room.

Julie Louise Paris looks as out of place sitting down on the cheap blue upholstered couch with her three thousand dollar shoes on a fifty dollar rug as she did standing on my

Mr. Charming (Not)

doorstep. She crosses her legs artfully, and those mossy green eyes land on me with a burning, single-minded intensity.

Yup. No one's eyes could be that green. Pretty sure she's indeed a robot bent on murder because I caused some kind of uproar by kissing her grandson.

Not that he's a stranger to scandal. Everyone at work knows all about Asher, so I'm not sure why I'm the one Julie Louise Paris had to hunt down. Maybe it's because I'm not a model, artist, actress, lawyer, doctor, heiress, professor, famous author, or even a designer. I'm just a manager of a small clothing company trying to make a difference in the world. I'm just me. Me, who lives in a regular, twelve hundred square foot house. And not a new one either. It was built in the seventies, which kind of shows. Me, who likes to play baseball with my brothers and can sometimes be coaxed into a game of flag football. Me, who loves thrifting, antiquing, and going to flea markets. Me, who has a closet full of our company's clothes because they're comfy and awesome, and none of them cost over a hundred dollars. Me, who wears regular runners and wipes my bottom with regular toilet paper, not the stuff spun from unicorn tears and elf's hair.

I'm so sure Julie Louise Paris is here to tell me off, fire me, and warn me to stay away from her grandson because she believes me to be a gold-digging, fortune-hunting, street-kissing hussy, that when she opens her mouth and speaks, I nearly face plant right off the couch.

Because those words sound something like this: "I want you to pretend to date my grandson."

"P...pretend to date him?" I choke out. *This* is the same grandson who is crazy rich, kisses like a kiss-devil himself, and from what I've seen of him in person and photos, is hot enough to incinerate me to a charred burned-up crisp with just a single glance?

If Julie Louise Paris is a fearsome, murderous robot, then her grandson is definitely a too good to be true, over the top hot, muscle upon muscle, fills out a suit like a dang fallen god, or maybe a risen demon, so hot that he'd fry his own circuits kind of robot.

The guy is over six feet of pure, well, sexy goodness. I still think he's spoiled, and it's weird that his granny buys him companies and fights his battles for him, but when I kissed him, I couldn't deny that bits of me—bits which hadn't seen the light of day for a good long while—woke to the sun spilling from him and were bathed in the golden glow of Asher Paris.

Wow. Get a freaking grip, Emily.

Getting out of my thoughts, I realize his granny is staring at me from the couch across the way. I'm on the matching loveseat, and I circumspectly cross my legs. If I were wearing any panties, they'd be damp. But I'm not because underwear ruins pajamas. Thank goodness for the extra layer of my old robe as it hides my body completely. Julie Louise Paris isn't able to tell that my nipples are so hard; they're practically ready to turn inside out. I seriously hope she can't see.

"Yes," she says in her cool, collected voice.

I'm pretty sure Julie Louise Paris has never been ruffled a day in her life, not even when she woke up to find that her grandson made it onto another magazine. And me with him. Why hadn't someone called me? Seriously. I should have heard about this by now. I don't live in a hole, despite what Julie Louise Paris must think of the house.

"D…date him? Why would I do that? And why fake?"

"Because." She blinks once. Twice. Her eyes never veer

away. That moss shade has to be unnatural. "I need Asher to settle down and settle in. I'm tired of the magazines, press, media, and scandals. I want them to stop hounding him. I bought this company, a little thing in the middle of nowhere, to give him a chance at a normal life. He's been working hard and he's even behaved these past six months. Everything was quiet and smooth until..."

Until me.

"But fake date him? That's...that's kind of insane."

Julie Louise Paris blinks again. Her eyelashes are unnaturally long, and the pink eyebrows and hair kind of throws me off, even though I've seen pictures. Nothing could prepare a person to meet someone like Julie in real life. Not that we're on a first-name basis. I shouldn't think of her like that.

"I need him to have a more wholesome image, but more than that, I want him to stay out of trouble. I want him to take this company seriously. Buy a house. And. Settle. In." She said that already. The settling. "What you did was very *unsettling*."

"I...I'm sorry. I shouldn't have. I don't even know why I...I was...my ex was..."

Looking uninterested, Julie waves her hand in the air, cutting me off. "Sweetheart, I'm sorry, but I have enough drama in my own life. I don't need nor want to hear about your ex. If he's an ex, that's a good thing because it means you're single and able to fake date my grandson. I want the whole world to believe he's finally met his match, and I want his life to be boring. So boring that the media knocks off and finds someone else to torment. I want him focused, and I want that company to thrive. Since you work there, you can show him the ropes and teach him a thing or two."

"I...but you don't even know me!"

"I know. But I can tell you're the hardworking sort of person who believes in fair trade fashion."

"How do you know that?" I'm not currently wearing any of it right now. It makes me wonder if those robot senses of hers are going haywire, and she can see through the walls in the house, all the way to my closet.

"You were wearing it in the photos. And anyway, I looked into you, of course. You have two degrees—community college, but still. You're a hard worker, and you've put in lots of unpaid overtime. You worked your way into a manager position, and the staff has nothing but good things to say about you. You also pay your taxes on time every year. You support three charities—two financially and a local animal shelter here, where you volunteer. Aside from that, you bought this house yourself, paid the down payment in cash, and you have zero debt aside from your car loan, which comes out of your bank account every month. You have two older brothers, both still living in this town. Your parents as well. You also graduated top of your high school class, and you got a hundred percent in English…"

"Wow." I cut her off but then have to swallow hard to get the boulder-sized lump in my throat to go down. "That's very thorough."

Julie Louise Paris—because I'm not using just her first name after a speech like that—smiles softly at me. She's less intimidating with her current expression, and she actually looks like she could be a nice person. Her eyes change, getting softer and shinier, and I can practically see the love flooding from her face like one of those token heavenly beams they're always depicting on TV.

"I really care about my grandson. People might see one side of him—the harder front he has to put on. They might

Mr. Charming (Not)

see a rich young man who has been spoiled, who has everything the world has to offer. A man who has spent years dating women. Dating. Many. Women. Many people think if you're rich, you're free game. That you have no feelings, emotions, or heart. They see just a glimpse and think they have the entire picture. Well, they're wrong. I want the world to see that Asher is a good man. He's got a good heart, and it's been broken more times than I can count. Not that he would ever confess to it. I want someone to treat him well. Maybe then he'd have some idea of what a relationship is truly supposed to look like."

"So, I could do that, but it would all be fake? That doesn't sound like what any relationship should be. I'm so confused. Why...seriously. Why would I do that?"

"Is it money you want?"

"No!" It's very obvious how insulted I am by that question.

"A promotion?"

"No."

"Fame?"

"Definitely not."

"What can I bribe you with to do this for me then?"

Suddenly, I realize Julie Louise Paris is no robot. She just looks like a grandma—a very fancy, pink-haired, mossy-eyed grandma who cares about their family. I know Asher is her only grandchild as I've done a bunch of research on them too—just what I could find online—when I found out she had bought our company. I feel slightly guilty about that now, but I'm not sure why. It was just a quick search—token stuff. I don't know what Julie Louise Paris got in her English class when she graduated.

"You're not going to threaten to fire me, bribe me, or ruin my life if I don't comply?"

"No."

"Hmm." I bite my lip hard.

"Hmm." Julie Louise Paris sits and waits, but then she can't contain herself, and after a minute, she blurts out, "I'll give you some money, but you can't tell Asher about it. He's going to ask you like it was his idea. I'll pay you ten thousand dollars if you agree. I'm sure you could use the money for something. Your family? Your house?"

"To date your grandson? For how long?" Why did I just ask that? It sounds like I'm starting to come around.

"Just a few months."

"A few *months*? That's crazy!"

"Fine. I'll make it double. Twenty grand. Don't turn me down. I'm a desperate grandmother who just wants to give her grandson a good life. You have no idea what it's like to be famous, to have money. To have everyone on earth wanting a piece of you."

"If I fake date him, wouldn't they want a piece of me too?"

Julie Louise Paris shakes her head. "You're too normal. Too boring. Too...too bland for them. They'd get tired of the whole thing after a week and leave him alone."

I'm so confused, but one thing I do know is that I'm not going to be bought. "I can't take money for that. I can't fake date someone. It's not...that's not right."

"Fine. You're fired then."

"What?" I leap up at the same time as Julie Louise Paris stands. "You can't do that! You said you wouldn't!"

"I own the company, dear. I'm sorry. I didn't want to have to resort to it, but you leave me no choice."

I've never used money to motivate me for anything, but right now, I know I have two choices. Take Julie Louise Paris up on her offer or lose my job and probably my house

Mr. Charming (Not)

and car too. My credit would be shit. Where would I work? Who would hire me? She'd probably make sure no one in St. Louis, or maybe the whole freaking country, or even beyond that, does.

She looks like a sweet old lady, but I think she might be the devil. Even if she does look really sad, a heck of a lot depressed, and totally deflated at the moment. Like she doesn't enjoy this bit at all. But whatever. She's the one doing it, not me.

"Fine," I seethe. "I'll take your twenty grand. And I want it in writing that you will never touch my position at the company. I don't need a promotion, but I want some certainty that you won't be able to fire me. That no one will. And that you won't mess with the company to get around it somehow."

"Deal." Julie Louise Paris sticks out an elegant-looking hand. She's not wearing any jewelry, but her fingers are slender and delicate, not twisted up or swollen at all with age. Her nails are filed into neat, tidy squares, but she doesn't even have them polished, let alone painted.

I don't want to shake her hand, but I find myself stretching mine out. She then clasps it with the lightest pressure. Shaking her hand is like shaking hands with a butterfly, and I'm kind of amazed that I just touched Julie Louise Paris. *The* Julie Louise Paris. But then I want to put my foot up my butt for being a little bit starstruck after what just happened here.

With a firm nod, Julie Louise Paris walks to the door, and I follow in her wake like I've been sucked into her tide.

"I'll have the money ready soon. Please don't tell Asher I was here or about the cash. If you do, our deal is void, and you will lose your job. I'm not a mean old lady. I swear I never wanted to threaten anyone, but I've lived sixty-five years on this earth, and I know that sometimes, unpleasant things can only come out sounding as unpleasant as they are. I'm sorry. I'm not trying to hurt you. I'm just trying to protect my family."

And with that, she leaves me. I sniff at the closed door, fighting back the pinpricks of tears. Why would I cry? Seriously. That's the last thing I should be doing.

It's just a lot. These past few days, Byron the bastard, my kitchen table, and kissing a complete stranger, who turned out to be my boss. Also, being threatened by his pretty, cute, sugary-looking, and hard as steel granny. She might look like a trendy, fashionable as fuck, sweetie, but really, she's more like a bad trip to the bathroom after one too many tacos.

Is this seriously what my life has become?

I stalk into the kitchen for a cup of coffee, but when I see the kitchen table still standing there, I know what I have to do.

4

EMILY

Here I thought that when rich people's kids and grandkids pissed them off by doing bad things and acting out, they just disowned and traded them in for a new batch. Clearly, I have a lot to learn. But if I could magically become the adopted granddaughter or daughter of a billionaire, I think I'd sign on that dotted line pretty fast. I mean, as long as everything is normal and I don't have to do weird or gross stuff for the privilege, which can probably be a whole list of nonsense things.

Then, I wouldn't need to worry about Asher Paris coming to my door and asking me to be his fake girlfriend, or his go-getter granny, who already bought my loyalty through bribery. I have to admit that I think it pained her to do it. She looked a little constipated when she threatened me.

I suppose the disowning route would have been easier for her, but I'm not walking in her super chic, ultra-expensive shoes.

Currently, I'm wearing a pair of ten-dollar high tops

that I thrifted last week, and they're totally worth more than ten bucks. I love funky shoes, and these happen to be in three different neon colors—yellow, green, and pink. Total. Freaking. Score. Glancing down at my shoes with a smile, I continue pushing a shopping cart down the aisles of a home improvement store as I look for the things I need.

In the aisle with cleaning supplies, I pick up a new plunger as well as a toilet brush since both of mine had to get thrown out last week. And no, I didn't have a plumbing problem because of uh…big logs. It was just time because they were ancient. Then, I amble down another aisle and get a pack of rubber gloves, tape, and some industrial glue before making my way to the garden section.

The yellow-handled ax with the big shiny head that I spot when I round the aisle is just right. I pick it up, testing the weight of it in my hands. It's so satisfying just to touch the thing and imagine how I'm going to use it. I place it in the cart and then wheel my way to the checkout.

The guy at the checkout is somewhere around twenty, and he has a shaggy blonde head with floppy blonde hair. He kind of reminds me of Byron, so he instantly leaves a bad taste in my mouth.

He eyes the cart and then eyes me up while he's ringing stuff in. "Looks like you're set there if you're going to be committing a murder."

A freaking what? Oh right. The ax.

I roll my eyes. "Not nearly." If this is his way of flirting with me, I can totally do without it. I'm now waiting for my boss to ambush me and ask me to fake date him, thanks to his granny. But before that, this is all thanks to Byron, his bullshit, and my freaking stupid kiss with Asher. "If I wanted to commit a murder, I'd be sure to grab more gloves, a full body paint suit, drop cloths, plastic sheeting, garbage bags, a hack saw, and oh yeah, a chain saw. Never underestimate their efficiency." The guy laughs, but it's slightly nervous. "Shit. I forgot the zip ties. The big, extra-strong kind. Can't have whoever it is escaping on me now."

"Um, that'll be fifty-two ninety," the guy mumbles, trying to avoid any eye contact.

Clearly, he's done flirting. In fact, he actually looks a little scared. I know I've already gone too far, but I can't help myself. "Good thing you don't know about the jerrycan in the back of my car." I wink as I slide my credit card through to pay. "Have a good one," I say cheerfully as the guy hands over my receipt.

I wheel the cart out, and I don't look back. When I get to the car, I pop the trunk, and yes, there really is a jerrycan back there. And it's full. I stopped for it before I went to the hardware store. If the guy is watching me, he's probably calling the cops right now.

Maybe I went too far.

I load my purchases into the trunk, and for once, I don't return the cart. I know it's seriously bad manners, but I feel all nervous now about the guy reading my plate number or calling the cops on me. I peel out of the parking lot with my heart hammering away, but I laugh at myself a few blocks later.

What happened to those days where the worst of my problems was losing to bots on games I have on my phone? These past couple of days have been complicated with all caps, as in COMPLICATED. And it all started with my breakup. Wait, no, that's not true. It all started with the stupid dining table.

When I get home, I pull into the garage and shut the door before opening my trunk. I don't want anyone to see me with a jerrycan and an ax. Yeah, now I'm the one who's paranoid.

Storming through the house, I slide open the back patio door, and the hot June air rushes in. I set the jerrycan outside so that the smell of gas doesn't keep twisting my stomach, and then I leave the door open because why not? My yard has a big fence all around it. No one can see me in here, in my kitchen.

The table eyes me defiantly as I lift the ax. "You're going down, motherplucker," I growl.

It says nothing in return, just taunting me with its nasty table of deeds. I guess it isn't its fault, but all I can see is Byron tupping that chick here. In my freaking house. On my table. I bought it years ago, so I guess it's not a total loss. Plus, I'm sure this is going to be therapeutic AF.

"Time for you to die," I mutter with as much sadistic glee as I can muster. I raise the ax above my head, channel my inner pissed-off lumberjack, and bring it down. Hard. The ax is sharp since it's brand new. And heavy. The table shudders under the first blow but doesn't give, so I swing again, narrowly missing the light fixtures in my haste. This time, the bastard crumples with a satisfying crunch. I step back, panting, and lower the ax down to my side.

Well then. I guess that was slightly anti-climactic, but there isn't anything I can do about it now. The table was no match for the ax, and it's not like it needs any more blows.

I set the ax aside, pick up two of the legs and a section of the top, and carry it outside. Then, I storm straight over the deck and paving stones to the fire pit at the far side of the yard. I do the same with the other section, heaping it on top of the small circle. I also have Byron the bastard's

Mr. Charming (Not)

clothes and shit inside that he didn't take. It's all junk, or I'd donate them. Really. Even if they had bad karma attached to them. But it's not even worth it. Basically, it's all just fit for a trash pile.

I heap all the crap on the broken table and go back for the jerrycan. I do keep it controlled since I don't want the fire department showing up, so I don't go wild with pyro glee and gas the whole thing such that the flames have the potential to reach twenty-five feet. I don't want the entire neighborhood seeing the fire, and I'm not trying to send up a distress signal, though god knows I could sure use one.

I'm actually quite frightened of fire, so when I say I put a little gas on the pile, it was literally just a few drops. The rest I'll save for my lawnmower. I go back to the house and return with the barbeque lighter. Gripping the lighter tightly, I get real close, light the table, and step back fast as the gas feeds the flame. It doesn't erupt. Also, there's sadly no mini-explosion or fire show, and the flames don't even really get going. Rather, they more like just flicker a shade. I'll probably, because I have the worst luck ever the past few days, have to light it like twenty times to get the damn table to burn.

Before I can consider the legality of burning a bunch of household junk in a tiny fire pit in my freaking backyard, the doorbell rings. And since the patio door is open, I can hear it clearly from out here. It's either the cops sent by the home store guy, wondering who I'm murdering in here, the fire department because someone saw smoke and phoned to report me already, or my future fake boyfriend.

I know it's not family or friends because they always text first. Always. I live quite far out, so everyone makes plans before randomly dropping by to see if I'm home. I suppose it could be the grandmother coming back to give me another old lady beat down, but I don't think so.

I think she beat her grandson by a few hours at most. I wonder where she flew in from. You know, on her broomstick. Ha. Just kidding. She probably has a private jet, and she probably came from somewhere exotic, though I think she lives in Paris. The fact that she chooses to live there means she likes it, which means her last name is probably a bunch of phony bolognas.

I hoof it fast to the front door. If it's not the grandson, my boss, the demon god of kisses, then I need to defuse the situation and fast.

The guy at the front door might be big and broad-shouldered, but he's no cop, and he's no firefighter. No, I don't have a uniform fetish, and that's not my fantasy. I'm just saying. Asher Paris does just fine in a tight heather gray t-shirt and a pair of faded jeans. Oh, and canvas shoes. High tops in black, which are nothing fancy. Totally ordinary, and no haute couture for him. Nothing to say his granny is one of the world's foremost, most famous, and one of the richest designers.

He crosses his arms and stares me down with eyes so blue that they rival the sky. Mountains probably take their granite ridges and trees their towering structure from Asher's face and body. His presence is like a clap of thunder right when a person thinks the storm has finally passed—the kind of thunder which reminds you that you're right in the heart of the eye.

I remember what his granny said about me not telling him about the money, which probably means she also doesn't want me to tell him that she was here at all, so I try and act surprised. "What are you doing here?" I squeak. "How did you know this is where I live?"

Mr. Charming (Not)

"Company records." He's not even the least bit ashamed of snooping into confidential files. Although, maybe they're not confidential since he owns the place. I'm not actually sure how that works.

If his granny hadn't primed me this morning, I feel like I'd be melting into a puddle of confusion right there on the doorstep. It might also possibly be a puddle of erotic juices. Just one glimpse of Asher Paris is enough to give my ovaries the jump start they need and get them purring for life.

Whatever. It was a very dry past three years. I thought I was physically compatible with Byron, but I had no idea. Because one kiss—one stolen kiss—with Asher, in which he was surprised and hardly trying, was the best kiss I've ever had in my entire life.

I can't imagine what the rest of him would be like.

I literally can't because that's too far. He's my boss. I know he's come to ask me to fake date him, but fake dating someone doesn't allow for thoughts about them in the sack. Jesus. I've never even thought of that term in my life. Under the sheets? In the hay? None of them are allowed. At least, I don't think so. I mean, I've never fake dated someone before, but I'm pretty sure that's how it goes.

I don't need a lecture on how most classical romances went from enemies to lovers or how marriages of convenience turned into blazing steamy pots of lusty satisfaction. I'm well aware, but this isn't the same thing as I'm not living in the eighteen hundreds here.

"Can I talk to you for a minute?" Asher is so smooth that his voice is like a purr. Not an angry tomcat yowl or a scuzzy whirring, but the kind of purr that makes my nipples so hard, I could have chopped the table in half with them.

"Umm." I think about his granny, those threats about getting fired, and how bullshit it is to get blackmailed by a sweet little senior citizen. Not to mention that it's galling to get dazzled by one's blackmailer because she's pretty fucking amazing all the way around. "Fine," I grunt.

I step into the house.

And walk into the living room.

I imagine we can talk. Have a nice little chat about getting all up and intimate. But not really, though. Because it's fake. So maybe set boundaries, guidelines, and rules?

Jesus, this is complicated.

If his granny didn't want him to know she was here, how is he on board with the fake dating idea anyway? She was so sure he would come here. Ask me. What did she say to him? Is she blackmailing him too, but he doesn't know it? Is he worried about getting written off? Maybe that's what rich people do, after all.

The living room is open to the kitchen on one side, which has a big patio door past the massive empty space my chopped-up table just left behind. Now there's a clear view of the backyard.

I was going to sit, but I stop dead right by the love seat. My mouth drops open, and I let out a little cry that sounds something like, "Fuck me sideways with a twenty-foot cactus."

Asher must find that some shade of amusing because he walks over and stands beside me. "Holy shit," he gasps. "Holy fucking shit."

"Yeah," I respond through a fog of numbness. "Yeah. It's bad."

"Bad? You call that bad? It's a grade-A disaster is what it is."

"I should phone."

Mr. Charming (Not)

"I would, but mine drowned yesterday morning."

"Okay." I finally snap out of my shocked stupor and pull my phone out of the back pocket of my jeans. I dial 9-1-1 as fast as my fingers will let me, which isn't fast at all. Shock is a curious sensation, and it makes me want to laugh in disbelief. It has to be disbelief because it's definitely not funny. It makes my fingers feel like they weigh a ton and are big bricks sewn onto my hand. And it also makes my brain move through a fog.

"Hello, operator." A female voice comes over the line, but I'm frozen and can't get a single word out.

Thank goodness for my future fake boyfriend. I guess my brain is still able to process that much. He plucks the phone from my hand and puts it to his ear, all smooth as a baby's bottom. Or is it supposed to be oil? Butter? Cold cream?

"Hello," Asher Paris says calmly.

He has a very nice speaking voice. And *it's* like butter. Real butter, on popcorn, and home popped. And not the stuff you put in the microwave. *Now I'm really losing it.*

"The emergency?" Asher continues.

He glances at me. Sky blues lock on my face, and now *I'm* butter. Christ, the fact that I'd fake date this guy even without the incentive of money or threats clearly says a lot about the new level of low I've just sunk to.

"The emergency, yes. Well, it seems like—I hate to say it—but the whole back section of our fence is on fire. Yes. Yes. I think a little bit of the side too." He shifts a step to the left and cranes his head. "Just a small fire. It got slightly out of control. Quite windy today. Yes. Thank you." He hangs up and passes me my phone. "The fire department should be here in ten."

I'm not all about the clichés. Truly. I actually hate them

with a burning passion of...well...my backyard fence, which is all on fire. Like, every bit of it. I'm not sure how Asher can stay so calm when there's a wall of flames out there.

But it appears that my life is going up in flames.

5

ASHER

Well, this certainly wasn't what I was expecting.

Sirens, firefighters, a backyard up in flames, and is that an ax in the kitchen?

I wait in the house, but only because the fiery goddess —perhaps literally—tells me to and skewers me with a gaze cold enough to freeze the flames erupting in her yard —this one not literally since we needed the firefighters.

I take a seat on one of the baby blue couches. It's an interesting choice of color. They're clearly supposed to resemble mid-century furniture, though they do a poor job at best. The house is ancient, probably built somewhere around the time my granny's designs took off, which was in 1974. I can tell spots have been opened up over the years. Someone attempted to do something with it, putting down laminate flooring and a new kitchen, though both seem to have been done at least twenty to thirty years ago. The updates are now outdated.

Well, enough about the house. I shift my attention back to the topic I've been using the house to avoid. Emily

Wellson. Yes, I know her name, as I really did go through the company files. I found her address there, just as I told her. No one tried to stop me because I did it during off hours, but even if someone was there, I don't think they would have denied me access to my own employee's information.

Emily Wellson. Age thirty-one. I know how long she's worked for the company and how she started as an assistant and is now a manager, but other than that, I know nothing about her.

I suppose I can add that she might be an ax-wielding pyromaniac, but maybe that's too harsh. Or perhaps it's not harsh at all. I'm a little bit nervous about dating a woman who lights things on fire in her backyard, keeps an ax in her kitchen, and kisses random strangers. Until a few minutes ago, I thought the last part was bad enough.

Christ. The dating might be fake, but I'll be lucky if I escape with my balls attached to my body. *Granny would love this.* She'd take one look at the backyard and laugh her butt off. She'd tell me karma has cold teats. I've given her a run for her money all her life, and so has my mom. I guess maybe it's coming back around to me.

Literally.

Because Emily steps through the back door, walks through the kitchen silently, and sits down across from me. I'm not sure how someone who just went through all that could offer such a stony expression. Her hair puts those earlier flames to shame. Her eyes are round, dark, wary, and furious, and her face, even sweaty and streaked with soot, is perfectly angelic. As she stares back at me, her bow lips remain flat and unsmiling.

"I know why you're here."

"Really?" I set one ankle on the other and stare Emily

Mr. Charming (Not)

down. Her eyes dart away quickly as she grabs a strand of lank, damp hair and twists it between her fingers.

"Oh. Um. I...I imagine it's about that kiss. I'm sorry. I ran and didn't come back to work to face you or explain. You're obviously here because you're confused. I'm—"

"You don't need to offer me an explanation." I really would like one, but I suppose we're past that now. I inhale deeply. There's still a hint of vanilla in the room, which I imagine Emily is responsible for unless she uses essential oils or air freshener. It also smells like out-of-control trash fire, but even that isn't hideous when it clings to a beautiful woman.

What the heck is wrong with me? Trash fire scent is not attractive, axes in kitchens are not sexy, and burning the neighborhood down should be sketchy at best. I've dated a lot of beautiful women, but I'm flabbergasted by the thought that none of them compare to Emily, even in her current state. There's just something different about her.

If by different I mean potentially criminal in the worst way, that would be correct.

"I do owe you one, though," Emily says, meaning the explanation. "I'm sorry. My ex was...he refused to leave. He made me come outside, and it was...well, you can imagine how it went. He said I would never be able to find someone since I'm apparently very under par, even though I was his one and only, the love of his life, and all that crap when he was living here. I was also funding his life, but anyway. I don't have a temper, but I saw red, and I just...I wanted to prove him wrong. This was also after he cheated on me by banging some stranger on my kitchen table, so it added uh...fuel to the fire."

Her face flames a shade to match her hair as she turns to look at the vacant spot in the kitchen.

I let out a sigh of relief when I realize what the ax was for. And the fire. She bought an ax, chopped up her kitchen table, took it outside, and burned it. That's not crazy. In fact, that's worthy of applause. And completely understandable.

What is not understandable is the wild urge I have to find her ex and tear him a new asshole. With the said ax.

I remember why I'm really here when Emily's gaze settles back on me. I feel my own ax growing firm—what?—in my jeans, so I shift my leg back down and slam my hands over my lap to hide it. It wasn't the reaction I was expecting, and I'm momentarily speechless.

"Dating," I blurt out like an idiot, and Emily's eyes get even wider. "I...when you kissed me, there were some media dogs there. They took some photos, and now it's everywhere. My granny..." Talking about being whipped by one's granny is enough to wilt anyone's, erm, excitement, so I subtly remove my hands from my lap. As they're quite damp from nervous sweating, I rub them down the length of my jeans. "My granny isn't pleased because she's tired of all the trouble I've caused her over the years. I promised her I'd behave, and this was one time where it wasn't my fault. I want to...to make the world believe that this wasn't, isn't, me being, uh, me, so I've invented a story, and I want you to play along."

"P...play along?"

"I can offer you an incentive. The story would be that we met before. I came to take a look at the company before my granny purchased it or something, and we fell deeply and instantly in love, but we wanted to keep a low profile because neither of us wanted the media attention. We dated secretly for the past six months, and now, this is the real reason I'm here. Because I couldn't stay away. I wanted to be at your side. I can't keep my hands off of you, clearly, and those photos were a private moment of joyful reunion that happened to be captured and splashed around all over the place. If we fake date for a few months, it should satisfy the media, and everyone will just move on and leave us alone. I'll go back to doing what I was doing, and you'll go back to, uh, well, your own life."

"Except we work together, and you're my boss. How would that not be as awkward as a trash fire getting out of control in my backyard and burning down my fence?"

I barely suppress a grin at her description, and I don't have to look out the window to see that she's in some serious trouble. "It wouldn't be."

"I just broke up with someone who I dated for years. I was even engaged to him. That would mean, if your story is true, I was cheating on him for six months. I can't do that. He's an asshole, but I just can't."

I think the guy deserves more than that. He deserves to be castrated with that ax in the kitchen, but I keep this tidbit to myself. "Fine. We'll figure something else out. Maybe we just met, and it was love at first sight. We'll date for a few months, everyone will move on, and then we'll quietly break up. No one will even notice because no one will be paying attention."

Emily huffs. She looks stunning when she blows hair out of her eyes and when her jaw sets in a determined line. "Except all my family and friends."

"They could know the truth. The people you trust."

She blinks. "Why would I do that? It's dishonest, and it's bound to be a mess. I think it could blow up in our faces. You're the one who made yourself a bad reputation. You should unmake it. By yourself."

I turn my attention to the backyard. "Rebuilding that

fence isn't going to be cheap. If your smoke damaged your neighbor's house, that's going to cost you. They probably gave you a fine too. Or something."

"Argh! So now you're just straight-up resorting to blackmail."

"No, I can help you. That's all I'm saying. I have money, and I have a lot of friends all over the place—people who can deal with this, so you don't have to." I try for my most charming grin, but at the moment, I feel like a greasy slime ball. She's right. Blackmail isn't exactly my style. "Plus, you'd get to stick it to your ex. He'd find out who you're dating. He made you feel like you'd never be good enough for anyone, and bam!"

Emily shakes her head. "That's a terrible reason."

"But it's appealing." I look pointedly at the ax in the kitchen until she has to turn around and look at it too. When she turns back around, she's scarlet again.

"Fine," she huffs. "But I want twenty grand, my backyard fixed, and the ability to tell my best friends and family that this isn't real. They'll all think I'm crazy, though, but maybe they'll already think so anyway. The last few days haven't been, uh, how my life normally goes. In case you're wondering."

"I wasn't." I stand and offer my hand. But she doesn't stand, and she doesn't shake it. Instead, she scowls at me like the plague just swept into her living room. "Alright, well, I have your number now, from the employee files. I'm getting a new phone today, so I'll call you tomorrow."

"Why bother? We see each other at work."

"Right. Just act...act normal. And don't answer any questions about me. People will be curious, and they'll ask you. Instead, just smile and shrug."

"Smile and shrug. That's your answer to this?" Emily hisses.

I smile. And I shrug. It's obviously quite effective since it earns me a steely look of disgust and nothing more. There really isn't anything to say to a smile and a shrug. Or maybe there isn't anything to say to what I just proposed.

I let myself out. Twenty grand. Well, twenty grand is nothing. I wonder what Emily needs the money for. Or wants it for. She could have asked for far more, and I would have given it to her. She probably sensed that I was somewhat desperate after I mentioned my granny and how I was giving her a hard time. Things like that add up. She could have figured I was getting disowned or something and that I would do anything to keep my fortune. Although it's not entirely true, disappointing my grandmother and having her think I broke my word to her is far worse.

Emily could have asked for more, but she didn't.

Now that she's going to be my fake girlfriend, maybe I'll get to find out why.

6

EMILY

I am so, so pooched.

The next day, I smile, smile, smile, and shrug, shrug, shrug my way through the long hours of whispered words behind my back, curious glances, and forward questions.

When Asher slips into my office and shuts the door behind him, I frantically scramble away from my desk. There aren't any windows in here, but I'm sure someone saw him enter. The scandal just keeps getting worse and worse. I want to fix it, but how can I? I've already sold my soul for somewhere around twenty grand, a backyard, and my job. Technically, I've sold it twice, so does that make me a double agent?

This is way too freaking complicated. Why did it have to be him that I grabbed and kissed?

Him. Asher Paris. I'm sure the entire workplace would secretly or not so secretly trade places with me in a second. Not just for the money, either. If Asher was a hobo, I think he could make a killing begging outside of anywhere. He'd just have to lean up against any building and flash his

Mr. Charming (Not)

disgustingly charming smile. Or maybe show off a little muscle, which any t-shirt and even the button-down dress shirt he has on right now would easily do. He looks even taller and broader in a freaking light purple shirt—yes, purple—and black pants. He exudes power and radiates bad boy vibes, even dressed like a boss.

It doesn't help that he has two freaking dimples on display, a face that would make even fairies and sirens weep, and dark hair that looks so rich and thick, it practically begs to be touched. Like a nice puppy or an extra soft kitty.

No. Asher is no puppy. And he's certainly no kitty. He's a blackmailing son of a beep who witnessed my ultimate humiliation twice now, snooped in my files to get my name and number, and is now my boss through the power of money and a generous granny. No puppy or kitty could do so much damage to my life.

Oh, and he's also my boyfriend—a fake one, but still.

"I was wondering if you'd like to have dinner with me tonight."

Those dimples dare me to deny him. Under any circumstances. Would I if my job wasn't at stake? Would I if I didn't need a fence and or have a neighbor threatening to sue me? Would I if his sweet little guard dog granny wasn't barking up my tail end?

My head screams no, but my ovaries scream yes, and isn't that just sickening?

"Dinner? Uh, I thought we should...that it would be better if we kept a low profile?"

"I'm not exactly sure what that is." There's that wickedly charming smile again. People like Asher prove that the world is a totally unjust place. No man should be given so many...assets. And dimples on top of it all.

"Well, I am. I don't want my photo taken and put in

magazines, and I also don't want anyone talking about me." I lower my voice to a hiss. "It's bad enough that everyone here is. I can feel it. They're all staring at me weirdly. They all think I'm that nasty cliché who bangs the boss. They also probably all think that soon enough, I'll be tossed aside, and won't it just teach me when I have to come back down to earth?"

"Holy pickles," Asher snorts. "That's a very depressing way to look at life. Are you always so pessimistic?"

"Are you always so un-pessimistic?" Maybe if he didn't like to have so much 'fun,' his granny wouldn't have come around threatening me, but also maybe half begging me to show him what something real actually looks like. Not that I'm going to do that. He's going to get some grudging friendship if he's lucky, and that's putting it nicely.

Asher shrugs. And smiles. I grind my teeth. "Alright, say we do it your way. Maybe that's what needs to happen to have everyone forget about me. Maybe if I make it clear I want to keep things private, they'll just quit."

"Doubtful. When you tell someone not to do something, it usually just makes them want to do it more."

Well, bloody fuck pants, isn't this a fine mess?

"I do want to keep things private as I'm not a very public person. And I still have to explain to my family and friends what's going on. Uh, I...if we're doing dinner, I'd rather cook." Did I really just say that? Offer an invitation to my house?

"That's great because I'm staying at a hotel, and it's not the kind that provides a luxury kitchen. Maybe I should change rooms."

"No! We can order in if needed." I'm definitely not going to get myself trapped in a hotel room. "To my place."

"Good. I have a surprise for you. It should be arriving at your house around five-thirty today. I assume you'll be off work and at home to sign for it by then."

"I hate surprises."

"Clearly. Especially after the backyard incident. Although, I'd call that more of a mistake, seeing as you didn't choose to surprise yourself by lighting the fire and letting it get out of control. Anyway, this is a good surprise. One you'll want."

I lower my voice and glance at the closed door. "What I want is for you to give me the money you promised and also give me assurance—signed assurance on a legal form —that my job is safe no matter what."

Asher's blue eyes flash. "What do you mean? You think I'd...that I would fire you?"

I remember what his granny said about him not knowing she talked to me. I almost gave it away yesterday and had to scramble to recover. Yet, here I am doing it again. "I...I don't know. I just want to be sure. I've worked here for a long time, and I do enjoy it. At least, I *did* before all the scandal and whatnot. If I lose my job, the money you'll give me won't matter. I need some assurance that this won't ruin my whole life."

He doesn't shoot back at me about how I should have thought about that before I locked lips with him so recklessly. Instead, Asher just nods. Honestly, I expected him to be more of an asshole, though it's probably coming. Guys like him are most assuredly always assholes. How can they not be? Having everything handed to you and the world at your disposal your whole life definitely wrecks most people.

"I'll have something on your desk by the end of the day.

And if you provide me with your banking information, I can transfer the money right away."

"Shouldn't we have some other sort of contract drawn up? About longevity or rules about faking it?"

"I trust you. A handshake would be enough for me."

"Do I have to spit on my hand first?"

Asher studies me, his face so handsome—even when it's purposely devoid of emotion—that my lady bits start pulsing. I'm wearing a skirt, and of course, underwear, and they're getting that uncomfortable damp sensation again.

"Swapping spit tends to get us into trouble, so maybe we should just shake without exchanging bodily fluids."

I swallow thickly. I wish I could say something smart to that, leave him with a lasting impression of my brilliance, but I'm pretty sure I've already left enough of an impression without trying. FML times twenty point eight.

"We'll shake tonight after dinner. And after we lay down some rules," Asher adds.

That makes sense. Here I was, ready to offer my hand like a dummy. I nod quickly and turn. Asher makes it out of my office before I even sit back down. When I do, I collapse into the chair so hard that it makes a strange belching noise at me.

I can't imagine what surprise Asher has in mind, and I'm almost afraid. Things have been going down the pooper pretty fast lately, so I don't trust my luck. My luck is about as good as the trash fire that happened yesterday. In fact, it's a pile of dung—a big heaping bowl of excrement. *Ugh, who would put that in a bowl? Lord.*

I check the time and realize I only have three hours to wait. I also have approximately that same amount of time to figure out how I'm going to handle Asher Paris tonight. At my house. Alone. With me. It shouldn't be a big deal as we're only fake dating, and it probably doesn't require anything more than the ability to lie, smile, and shrug.

With a heavy sigh, I lean back, shut my eyes, and tell that to the goosebumps which just broke out all over my body.

7

ASHER

I've kissed a few women before. A gentleman doesn't kiss and tell, so I'll just say it *might* have been a little bit more than a few. With my more than limited experience, I'm not sure why I can't get that kiss with Emily out of my mind. It wasn't even real. She was just doing it to get back at her ex, and it had zero premeditation or any lead-up to it.

And yet.

Maybe that's what made it more meaningful.

I don't know, but I do know that when I pull up to her house, things feel different. We're only fake dating, and we're going to talk about a list of rules. I'm seriously not here for any other reason since I basically bribed her into this.

And still.

I climb out of the car and glance around. As far as I know, I wasn't followed. There aren't any photographers or skeezy vans sitting at the curb, awaiting my arrival, which is already a good sign. Maybe once they did some research after breaking the kiss story and found out that Emily is just a normal person, they gave up. Perhaps they're just waiting for my next scandal, confident I'll have moved on in a week or two.

It makes me feel like a real butthole—a dirty one at that—to realize those thoughts are probably true. That's how I've dated in the past.

No wonder my granny says I'll put her in an early grave. If I had a kid like me, I'd probably be spouting off the same. And she also had my mother to contend with for the past forty-some odd years as well.

I feel nervous as I walk up to the front door. It's after six, so I'm sure my surprise has already arrived. When I knock on the door, I'm even more astounded to have Emily rip it open and snarl at me as if I've just been caught red-handed trying to light a kitten on fire.

"How could you get me this?" she hisses, her lips pulled back. "Seriously?"

There's only one thing to do in a situation like this. In most situations, actually. Shrug. And smile. "Whatever I did, I didn't do it on purpose. Personally, I thought it was a nice gesture."

"*Personally,* you can shove your surprises up your hind end." Emily spits out, but then she moderates her expression when she notes my confusion. "I mean, thank you. Thank you for the table. I really do appreciate it. It was very kind of you to replace my last one. But, as you know..." She looks behind me, grips me by the front of my dress shirt, and hauls me inside. Then, she slams the door after I stumble in. I've lost my ability to shrug, and my smile has been wiped away to be replaced by surprise. Emily is somewhere around five-six and probably a hundred pounds, and she just dragged me in like I'm a toothpick myself.

She throws her hands on her hips. "I wanted to say that

since you know I'm single now, the surprise isn't a very good one."

"Why is that?" I'm still really freaking confused here. I've given a lot of gifts in the past, mostly purses, shoes, dresses, jewelry, the usual, and most women enjoy receiving them.

Granted, I've never given a table before. I should have known better. Emily looks at me like it should be obvious. "Because! I have no one to help me put it together. It's in like ten thousand pieces, still right where the delivery guys dropped it off."

"Oh."

"Oh?"

"I didn't think of that. Really, I thought it would come assembled."

"That would have been nice."

"I didn't realize, or I would have ordered it as such. Or paid for someone to come do it."

"I have brothers, but they don't live here. My parents do, but, uh, they're…my dad is…okay, this is really embarrassing, and he'd kill me if he heard me say it, but he's not very um…"

"I understand." She's trying to say that her dad isn't very handy, which is obviously hard for her. She clearly loves her parents a lot and doesn't want to embarrass them even though they're not here and will never know.

Emily saws at her bottom lip until it turns a dark, alluring shade of red. My dick notices and offers his help as a hard tool of persuasion to help put the table together. Evidently, the bastard influences my brain.

"I could do it if you'll help me. It most probably needs a second set of hands."

She looks me up and down and barely manages not to

snort. "Uhmmm...I have like, no tools. I just have this token box my parents assembled and gave to me as a gift when I bought the house."

"That should do it. Anything else it needs should have come in the box."

"Oh. I...well..."

I arch a brow. "Is it that you don't want my help, or after hacking the last one to bits and setting it on fire, you didn't want a replacement? I'm sorry if I've overstepped here or was presumptuous."

"Presumptuous?" Emily gapes. "You use that word?"

"I do."

"Do you...do you read classics?"

"Happily or unhappily? Have I or would I in the future when not pressed to do it for some sort of class?"

"The latter."

"I suppose I do." I can practically feel my cock trying to reach through my pants and cock me right in the jaw because admitting that sounds a little bit, eh, less than macho. Instead, I should have said, "No, I only like to read about sports and business, and then watch sports, play sports, and do things sports-related, especially violent, rough, manly sports like football or rugby. Or like strong man competitions."

But maybe I'm wrong because Emily breaks into a grin and looks at me with newfound respect. And maybe there's even a touch of admiration in there too.

"Really?"

"I suppose."

"You suppose? Well...I guess we'll have one thing in common other than that we work together, at the very least." She hesitates but then turns and motions over her shoulder. "Come on. We'll look at the table. Maybe we'll even get it assembled."

I hope it's the kind that stands up to being used and doesn't just look pretty but falls apart with one hard breath in its direction. I desperately hope I'm not going to embarrass myself and fail at this because I haven't put together a damn thing since shop class in high school. My mom didn't give a rat's bottom end where I went to school, and Granny wanted me to go somewhere as normal as possible, so yes, I did shop class. I did woodworking, motors, and welding, thank you very much. That was a *long* time ago, though. Men also tend to be directionally challenged, but in our defense, most of those directions are written out like pure confusing trash.

When I get to the kitchen and see Emily standing in front of a massive box which has been opened, the lid lifted, and a piece of furniture that's in more pieces than the last one which met its end by ax and fiery doom, I have to tamp down my rising sigh. Emily's eyes are all large and shining with hope. My balls tighten up furiously as I realize I don't want to let her down.

I can't let her down. For her. And for me.

This is quite possibly, technically, *maybe* my first task as a fake boyfriend, and I will *not* fail at it, even if it takes me three days to put it together, working round the clock.

"Rules," Emily blurts as I kneel down before the box of parts. "We need rules."

I reach for the instruction sheet. *How the heck is this thing ever going to turn into a table? And where's the instruction sheet that's supposed to come with my new girlfriend? My* fake *girlfriend.*

"I agree."

Emily kneels beside me, eyeing the box, and a sudden

Mr. Charming (Not)

sweet rush of delightful and soft feminine scent follows in her wake. This is something I haven't had the pleasure of inhaling before. Something unique—in a world where everyone dress and look the same—that makes my balls stir again. I drag in another deep breath, filling my lungs with it while my brain works overtime, trying to determine what exactly it is.

Is it ginger? I think that's the spicy part at the start, but the undertone is sweet. Something like grapefruit, or maybe it's lemongrass, all combined with the richness of vanilla.

"So, what are they?"

I stare blankly at the instruction sheet. There are approximately six thousand steps on there. How could something that costs so much money still require assembly? For what I paid for this table, it should have come complete, serving up its own dinners on gold plates with gold knives and forks.

That would be nice. For dinner to spontaneously put itself on the table and for the table to chef up its own magic. In my world, that's called takeout, but there's no magic in choosing something off a menu and dialing a number.

"Uh...rules. Right."

"You're not even paying attention!" Emily snatches the table instructions out of my hand. She gets close, and I inhale deeply again. My groin appreciates the mystery of the scent as much as my olfactory senses do. She glances at the paper, then reaches into the box and pulls out two metal pieces that are obviously part of the legs.

"I am. Sorry."

"Sorry my ass."

"You have a very fine one." The words are out before I

can consider them, and while my brain says it's true, Emily's look is absolutely scalding.

"Rule number one: No comments about my ass or my assets. Rule number two: They're off-limits. Forever. Always. Rule number three: This is fake. On the odd chance that you have to do something in public, then it's hand-holding or a brush of the shoulder. Never anything more. Rule number four: Never anything at work. We're professional there. Always. I don't want this messing with my job any more than it has. And lastly, rule number five: When we have to spend time together, we find something else to do. Bring your own entertainment, as in your work, your phone, or a book."

I look over Emily's shoulder, past the delicate, pretty column of her neck and all that fiery hair to the paper in her hand. Then, I reach for the next couple of metal parts. I have to take one of the parts Emily is holding, and when I do, our hands brush, but we don't create sparks. Well, unless my dick rising to life at the appreciation of the briefest of brushes over silky skin counts.

"You mean like this?"

"This is not entertainment. I'm busy, and I have my own life. Part of this agreement should not be me having to keep you busy. This isn't a real relationship, and honestly, I'm just glad to get out of the last one. I'm tired of having to support someone, cook their meals, do their laundry, and find things to do to keep them from being bored because they honestly couldn't have enough of a life to bother with actually finding hobbies of their own—" She cuts herself off and makes a noise in her throat. "Sorry. That sounds bitter."

"No. No worries. You won't have to cook for me, clean

Mr. Charming (Not)

for me, do my laundry, or support me financially. And I have enough hobbies of my own."

Emily hesitates, but then her eyes flick down to the paper, and she grabs another part out of the box. I let my eyes linger on her face. I've forgotten all about the table. Rather, I'm quite transfixed by this woman's beauty. She has a wounded air, thanks to her douchebag of an ex, and it sounds like she was quite ill-treated by the scumbag, lowlife, sponging loser who had zero appreciation for the actual person she is. He obviously used her like his mama's basement and lived accordingly. And then cheated on her to boot. It shouldn't be too hard to follow up to such a vile creature, but it's because the act was so nauseating that winning Emily's trust is going to be extremely difficult.

So, I'll follow her rules. It shouldn't be hard at all, given that this isn't real, but her physical proximity combined with the beauty she doesn't even seem to be aware of is doing things to me. *Those* kind of things. Things that are hard to ignore.

I already wonder what it would be like to kiss her. No, I know what it was like. But I wonder what it would be like to do it again, without the element of surprise. Or maybe with it, but somewhere less public and with far less agenda.

Emily stabs at the paper. "This makes no sense." Her eyes narrow, and when her teeth sink into her plush lip again, I nearly let out a groan. This is going to be a hang dang of a lot harder than I anticipated.

"I think you actually need this piece." I lean past her toward the box and pull out a different part of the leg. "Not that one."

"Oh." She frowns, her brow creasing up with worry lines I'd like to smooth away. The urge makes no sense because I can't remember ever having it before. Or noticing something like that. "You're right."

She fits the two pieces together, grabs the next two, and the first leg begins to take shape. Maybe this will be easier than I previously thought. The table, I mean. Not fake dating a woman I'm noticing things about that are a first for me. I'm not a thoughtless person, but suddenly, I realize I've never fully taken the time to want to know those superfluous things about a person. I've always been too busy...well...doing *other things* with them.

I quickly assemble the second table leg so that I feel like less of an asshole. Is it possible I was just like Emily's ex? Not using someone or sponging off them for money, but the fact that I never even bothered with truly getting to the heart of anything at all?

Of course that was me. But to be fair, I got a lot of it in return. The women I dated weren't looking for something permanent, and they didn't want a deeper connection. What they wanted was what I wanted—companionship for a short term, and by companionship, I don't exactly mean the hand-holding kind. To be blunt, no one was thinking about love.

I guess I've always been too realistic for that.

Because of the money.

Because of my name.

Because I was raised to believe that things like love are just a fantasy. I watched my mom suffer for it, over and over again, and I had a much more practical granny who, since I was a kid, told me that love is neither here nor there and might not exist at all.

"Are you okay?"

I shake myself out of my not-so-pleasant memories and find Emily's forehead creased again. She's looking at me, and all her worry is for me now. Not *because* of me, but *for* me.

"Yeah. Just jetlagged. A lot's happened in the past few days."

"You're telling me." She grins, and god, I'd like to see that smile again, with less self-deprecation and more authentic joy. I'd like to be the one who puts it there too, but cracking a stupid joke wouldn't count.

I make sure I keep my attention focused on the table, and after forty minutes, we actually have something that looks complete. It's modern with a dark stained top and curving dark metal legs. Honestly, it looked better online. I chose something for Emily because it was easy for me to find something I liked and click a button to have it ordered to her house to fill the space where her last table stood.

But I never asked her what *she* liked.

If she hates it, she feigns joy well enough. Maybe she's just happy that the wretched task of putting it together is complete. Either way, she darts off, and I hear her calling for a pizza. At least she doesn't ask me either before she orders. She just gets what she wants and makes it an extra-large, enough for both of us. She's thoughtful while daring me to take it or leave it.

When the pizza arrives—the world's fastest delivery—she pays and takes it to where I'm cleaning up the debris from the table. The box that contained the table parts is huge, and I've been folding it up, trying to figure out where I'm going to stuff it. I'm anticipating a brown bin outside or perhaps a blue one for recycling because making origami with thick cardboard is a lot harder than it sounds.

Emily walks past me and places the pizza box on the table.

We both hold our breath at the same time. When

nothing happens, she steps into the kitchen to get a roll of paper towel while I move the folded-up box out of the way.

The table holds for one solid minute.

Then it collapses in on itself, depositing legs, the wood plank top, and our dinner into a heap on the floor.

8

EMILY

The worst part about having a fake boyfriend is that I have to actually pretend to be dating him. I mean, I guess that's the point of any boyfriend. You have to physically force yourself to hang out with them. Or, in the case of the lucky few out there who are deep in the starry realms of true love, they might actually want to hang out with their significant other.

Two days after the table incident, when Asher emails me of all things, asking me if I want to see a movie, I feel like I can't say no. It's a public outing, but it's not so public that people would be following us around. Certainly, photographers can't just sneak into a theatre whenever they want, and they'd no doubt have to use flash or something, which would be totally disruptive. I figure it's innocent enough, so I respond with the name of a huge theatre and a show that looks like it would for certain be terrible but also draw a big crowd.

I don't want us to be the only ones in the theatre, and I don't want Asher to get any ideas. There isn't going to be any sneaky slipping of an arm around my shoulders, sharing popcorn or drinks, and no swapping spit.

My inbox flashes a new message, so I open and read it quickly. Apparently, Asher is excited about my choice of movie, and of course he would be. It's some token action thing. He did leave it up to me to choose, and I can't remember the last time anyone did that. Certainly, Byron the bastard never would have let me choose. There was no way he'd ever go for anything other than crap action, and I hated it. I realize that in all the years we dated, we only saw two movies together. Most of the time, I'd go with my friends, and he'd go with his.

That's basically how we did a lot of things.

I wrench around in my chair and face the back cabinet of my desk. My eyes are stinging and prickling like they've gone rogue cactus on me. I'm tearing up because I just realized what a waste the past three years of my life were. I mean, partner-wise. I can't even call it a love life because it wasn't really that.

Why was I going to marry the guy?

I know the homeless guy I gave my ring to was delighted with it. He's probably the only one who got any real joy out of the thing. Would I seriously have gone through with an actual wedding? I got engaged six months ago, and I never even started to talk about setting a date. That should have been a good indication that I didn't really want to get married. Byron, as usual, probably just wanted a free ride. The engagement ring was the only gift of any value he ever bought me. It was cheap, which was fine by me, but it seriously wasn't my style, which said that Byron didn't know me at all. He could have bought me something cheap yet still nice. Like a vintage piece off of a used site or

Mr. Charming (Not)

something, which I would have been plenty impressed with.

"I am such a wreck," I mutter under my breath. Doubly so because now I've downgraded to a fake boyfriend instead of a real one in order to save my butt.

Okay, so maybe he's hotter than any boyfriend I've ever had, real or otherwise. He's basically like a walking ice cream cone with triple scoops of cherry cheesecake ice cream. Meaning he's good enough to lick.

He might not be able to put a table together, but my dad couldn't have done it either, and I don't think less of him. To be honest, the table might have been because of me. It could have been the parts I'd done that made it collapse. Asher wanted to have another go at it, but I told him to leave it. I also had to clean it up since it was covered in gooey cheese and messy pizza sauce.

I spin back around, the tears crisis averted, and dedicate my attention to killing the next two hours before I can go home and kill an hour before my date that's not a date.

Those hours fly by, and before I know it, my doorbell is ringing, and I'm hopping on one foot to answer it while pulling on the sixth pair of jeans I've tried on and discarded. It's just my luck that choosing an outfit for a fake date is no less difficult than choosing something for a real one.

I make sure my ripped-up skinny jeans are firmly and properly in place, and I also check to be sure that my shirt—an oversized flowy thing that looked great on the mannequin at the store but one I still have my doubts about because it fits really freaking weird, and it was also expensive, so I feel like it's a crime not to wear it—is properly fitted and not exposing any bits and pieces. Namely, my nipples.

Fake dating does not include nip slips.

I should add that to the list of rules.

Asher looks incredible, and he's wearing jeans too, paired with a flannel button-down. He looks so casual yet extra cherry cheesecake ice-creamy, which makes him look extra tasty.

Extra tasty? Am I even listening to myself? Way to objectify him. Or rather, foodify him. Whatever. It's still wrong no matter what term is used.

I try to ignore the bulgy bits of him and focus on the more streamlined areas. Those ultra-wonderful jet blue eyes flash as they rake over me. "I like that shirt," he says. Because, of course, he would.

"Your grandma is a famous designer. Also, I can see straight through your compliments about my wardrobe. Even though this shirt was stupidly expensive, it's still bought at the mall. It's not fast fashion, though, in case you were wondering. I'm much too conscientious for that now."

Asher's grin is far too easy and comfortable. Like he's at home wearing it, and gosh, does it ever look incredible on him. "I'll amend what I said then. That shirt looks good on *you*." His eyes focus on my chest, and for a second, I'm sure a nip slip has happened after all.

I self-consciously crank my head down, but nope. Everything's well covered.

"Shall we go? I can drive us if that's alright."

I don't know if it is, but I grab my purse from beside the door anyway. I feel frumpy next to all that godliness walking beside me, but Asher doesn't even notice. He opens the car door for me like I'm a princess and even shuts it too.

No one has ever done that for me before.

Between the silence that doesn't get filled, Asher's deli-

Mr. Charming (Not)

cious smelling cologne, and his nearness taking up the entire car, which is a good-sized sedan, and he's technically not that close, I'm so nervous that my shirt is damp by the time we get to the theatre.

Yuck. Nothing like being an un-hot mess.

Asher buys the tickets and gets us two popcorns and drinks like he read my mind or magically knew the unspoken rules about sharing. Because sharing means that our hands might accidentally brush, which would be devastating because the fewer accidental touches we have, the better. I think. I mean, yes, yes, I'm certain about that.

The theatre is packed, and we have to squeeze down a row of people to get to our seats. Asher is right beside me, but I take care to lean as far to the right as possible, over to a big sweaty guy who is wheezing with every breath and smells like a cross between old cheese and motor oil. He has a huge black beard, and I think I can see something moving around in there. As in, some kind of insect or something.

Still, I swallow down my revulsion at the beard of horror and lean in his direction because it's better than leaning into Asher. By better, I mean safer because then, my hormones are less tempted to riot and pitch a full-on revolt that ends with me frantically kissing him again.

My nipples are now so hard that they're practically piercing through the bag of popcorn I have cradled against my chest, and the movie hasn't even started yet.

Thank fuck, it finally does after a few excruciating minutes, and the theatre is also full by the time the lights go down.

I throw myself into devouring popcorn, which isn't hard because I haven't had dinner yet, and I'm starving and also watching the world's most cheesy action-packed D-grade movie. I honestly think the guy's beard beside me is more interesting, though interesting in an incredibly nasty sort of way. There's more action going on in there than on the screen.

The movie is about twenty minutes in, and I'm wondering how the heck I'm going to get through the rest because it is bad with a big sheep-like sounding 'baaaaa-d,' when Asher makes a strange noise. It sounds like he's choking on a popcorn kernel, and I turn so rapidly that I nearly spill mine all over Mr. Crawly Beard's Lap. I apologize in whispered tones and maneuver myself more carefully.

It's pretty dark in the theatre, but I can see that Asher's face is purple. As in choking, I can't breathe, and I'm near death kind of purple.

"Holy god," I hiss. "Are you okay?"

His jaw clenches, and I swear his right eyeball ticks. "Yeah."

At least he can talk. If he can talk, then he's not choking, and he's not going to die. But why is he such a horrible color? It's not hot in the place. In fact, it's nicely air-conditioned. "Are you sick?"

He shakes his head, but it's too fast.

"Oh my god, are you allergic to popcorn? Or…or soda?"

"No."

"Maybe they put peanuts into the butter or something. Are you allergic to nuts?"

"No."

"Strange oils?"

"No."

"Butter that's not really butter?"

"No."

Mr. Charming (Not)

"Are you allergic to anything? Maybe someone's wearing something in here that's doing it."

"No."

He doesn't shrug. Or smile. And that's probably a bad sign. Also, his face brightens and turns into a deeper shade of plum, which is seriously not good.

"Are you sure you're not sick? Is your tummy okay?" I can't believe I just asked him if his tummy is okay. Jesus. Mark that one down on the list of humiliating questions not to ask someone you barely even know. If this were a real date, I'm sure I wouldn't have a second one.

Maybe that's what I need to do. But as tempting as it is, no, I can't do that. I can't purposely drive him away. His grandmother will come down on me like a ton of bricks and freaking fire my ass, which would then really suck. So, for now, I have to ride this out.

"I'm good," Asher grinds, but his voice sounds highly constipated. I mean, not like I've met that many highly constipated people, but it just sounds all pinched and wrong. Plus, he looks even worse. Now he's biting his lip, and his nostrils are flaring.

"Are you in pain?"

He doesn't answer that. Instead, he shoves his bag of popcorn at me and says, "I'll be right back." Then, he stands right up with absolutely no care for the rows of people behind us, but we're also right in the middle of the theatre, in the middle of a row, so I'm not sure how else he is supposed to get out.

He makes quick work of it, nimbly dodging past at least fifteen people. When he hits the aisle, he makes a break for it and disappears around the corner so fast that I have to blink at his empty seat.

Holy freaking popcorn. I have no idea what just happened.

I don't think it was normal, though, so I should go and check if Asher's okay. He might not be my real boyfriend, but he is my boss, and I do kind of know him. Besides, I'm here with him either way, so I feel kind of responsible for his wellbeing.

I'm also slightly freaked out.

Plus, I'd really like to get away from Crawly Beard. Just saying.

I stand up too and make apologies down the entire row as I try to climb out. I'm not freaking athletic and nimble like Asher, so I struggle a little. Plus, I'm holding two bags of popcorn and two full drinks. I'm a walking disaster.

Finally, I manage to get out of the theatre, and the first person I see, coming out of the washrooms at the end of the hall, is Asher. Thankfully, he's no longer purple. Now, he's a perfectly normal color, at least until he sees me, then his cheeks become slightly pink.

"Are you alright?" I ask as soon as he's close enough that I can whisper and know he'll hear me.

He nods, but then he runs a hand through his dark hair, ruffling it in a messy, sexy kind of way that makes my fingers, nipples, and va-jay vibrate.

"I'm glad you look better. You scared the crap out of me."

"I'm sorry."

"Are you sure you're okay?"

Asher gets that weird look I've seen on my brothers' faces way too many times when we were growing up, and they did something terrible they knew would piss my parents off. He looks guilty, and I have no idea why.

I lower my voice to a whisper. "You know we're just fake dating, right? If something's going on..." I'm the one who feels sick saying it, though. Thinking about him rushing

Mr. Charming (Not)

out of the theatre to answer a text from someone else, someone female who is not me, really sucks.

"No. It's not that."

I believe him. Irrationally, of course, my relief is immense. "If you're feeling sick, you can just tell me. I'm not one of those people who is all uptight and will freak out. I can even drive you home if you want, or at least back to your hotel, and get a cab. Or if you need to go to the doctor, I can—"

"It's not that. Really. I'm fine."

"But you...you just *ran* out of there."

Asher gets that look again, but this time, I realize it's not guilt. It's embarrassment. I remember he was coming out of the washrooms. *Oh. It was that kind of problem.*

"You realize I grew up with two brothers. There really isn't any bathroom humor I haven't heard. They used to take very pointed and specific pleasure in farting on me. They'd freaking hunt me down in the house, walk into a room, find me there, come over, and fart straight on me. Both of them. They were disgusting beasts. I swear it was the only thing that gave their life meaning. Of course, me being their little sister, they felt they had a right to initiate me into life that way."

I watch carefully, and Asher's shoulders slump. His jaw relaxes, and his left eye stops ticking. The vein in his forehead also stops throbbing, but his cheeks become an even darker red. He blows out a long breath.

"We had a lunch meeting. Tacos. I've, uh, well...the beans and spices were...potent. I didn't want to, um, pass gas. In front of you. Or in a public place."

I can't hide my amusement, literally. Unable to help myself, I giggle. I know I shouldn't laugh because Asher's so serious and mortified, but yeah. I did grow up with two brothers, and their whole world revolved around gas.

"It's good to know that even billionaires get gastric catastrophes."

"That's not funny. Being rich doesn't give you a steel stomach."

"It should give you better immunity. You can afford better quality food, good vitamins, and the best medical care."

"That's more after the fact."

"So you're not immune to bad tacos?"

Asher frowns. "They were actually quite good."

Suddenly, I'm worried I'm being rude and that I've insulted him. I shouldn't have made that comment about his money. Jesus, that was the ultimate in tactlessness. Then I insulted his lunch, too. I'm about to apologize when I see that the lines around Asher's mouth have deepened. Not the frown or grimace lines, but the smile lines. He's used to doing that. Smiling, I mean. I blink at him, and I'm sorry to say, but I'm also suddenly seeing him as a person for the first time. I mean, not as some immensely rich guy with a famous grandma, an intimidating figure, a powerful man, or even as my boss. He's just a person who eats tacos and gets gassy like everyone else.

A person who is alarmingly close to me and just as alarmingly attractive. I'm a little shocked at his height. I knew he was tall and broad, but it's like my senses are just now fully registering his physical magnificence. I notice the way a strand of his dark hair is mussed and is curling over his left ear. I study his rugged jawline and gorgeous lips, and I can't believe I was ever daring enough to have grabbed and kissed him.

"Uh, yeah, so farts," I mumble, searching for something

to say to cover up my blatant perusal. "Yes. Well, my brothers, as I said, it was basically their whole world. My mom got so mad about all the fart talk that she actually banned the word in the house. We all had to call it fluffing. My brothers took that as a challenge and made up a code name for all their farts. As well as the classifications. My mom created monsters with her desire for politeness. They had The Bedding Fluffer, which was code for a Dutch oven, The Floatlining Flatulence, aka the silent but violent, the Gargantuine Gasper..." I trail off, now embarrassed that I'm just standing here talking about this.

Asher looks more than mildly amused, though. "It sounds like you had a great childhood."

I can feel myself blushing. "I did. Do you want to get out of here? Maybe go for a walk somewhere?" I can't believe I just put that out there. I should have just asked if he could take me home, but then I feel like he'd feel bad about ruining our date night that's not even a real date night.

I curse myself for being way too nice.

Suddenly, Asher reaches out, and it takes me a second to realize he's not reaching for me. Of course he's not reaching for me. But at the thought of it, my stomach still cramps, my thighs quiver, and my nipples nipple, I mean, shit, pucker. He then plucks his popcorn and his drink out of my arms. I barely even realized I was still holding anything.

"That would be nice. I'm glad I didn't ruin the movie for you."

"You didn't ruin anything." God, I wish I could be mean. I wish I could tell him that he ruined my entire night, dang it, and we'd better call this whole dating crap off. Then ask if he could still take care of my backyard and if I *might* still have some job security. But I can't. I just can't. No matter how much I want to. All that comes out is a hiccup, followed by a tiny laugh. "It was pretty bad, wasn't it?"

He nods. I nod. He shrugs. And then, of course, he smiles and shrugs. And all I can do is follow him out of the theatre.

9

ASHER

The popcorn honestly isn't that good, and the soda is flat. I pitch mine into the nearest garbage can outside, and Emily does the same. I was stunned that she wanted to give me another chance. She could have just asked me to take her home. I'm pretty sure any other woman would have called me disgusting, deemed the night ruined, and demanded cab fare because they didn't want to gamble being in an enclosed space with me after the taco gas fiasco.

The theatre area is busy, with a strip mall surrounding it and restaurants bracketing the area. The parking lot is also jam-packed. I don't know the area, but Emily saves me again.

"There's a park five minutes or so drive away if you wanted to go walk there."

A park. It's a nice suggestion. It's not quite dark yet, but the sun will be setting soon. It's a rather romantic setting, and I'm not sure if she realizes it or not. However, the fact that she quickly turns away from me and power walks to the car suggests she does. She doesn't correct herself, though, and I'm not sure if she just wants to save face, if she's taking the faking thing seriously, or if she's too shy. She also has an excellent memory, which is a good thing for me because I'd already forgotten where I'd parked.

I hold her door for her again before walking around the car and getting in at the driver's side.

Driving down the street while she gives me excellent directions, I miss my cars. I flew into St. Louis and rented a sedan because they didn't exactly have imported sports cars on their list of choices. I'm debating about flying back to LA, getting one of my cars, and driving it back here just so I have it. I could buy another, but there are ones I love driving because they're mine. I don't want something new. Rather, I want something familiar because I get used to the way a car handles. How it hugs the road, how it accelerates—that kind of thing. That's what I miss.

Also, having a real home. The hotel thing, after just a few days, is already getting old. "I have to find a house," I blurt. "Soon. I can't stand the hotel anymore. Any recommendations in the area?"

Emily snorts. "Yeah. Right." She doesn't look at me as she keeps focused on the traffic ahead. Not fearfully like I might plow into someone but in an interested—*I'm giving you directions so I can't tear my eyes away because if I mess up, it's going to be humiliating*—kind of way. "I wouldn't know what any of the neighborhoods in your price range are like. I've never even driven through them as most of them are gated communities. I would suggest an online search. Just type an amount in the price bracket with six zeroes behind it. That should do it."

"Just because I have money doesn't mean I want to live in a mansion."

She does look at me now, totally shocked. "I just

assumed you'd want to live in something, erm, comfortable for you."

That basically translates into her hinting how she knows what my house looks like in LA because there's this thing called the internet, and anyone can find out that kind of information. She probably also knows what my penthouse looks like in New York, what my flat looks like in London, Paris, our family vacation house in Milan, and so on.

"I was wondering if you'd like to come with me."

"No!" Panic tightens her features. "If someone happened to be spying on us, that would give off the worst impression. Like we're thinking about moving in together after just meeting each other. That would be the story of the year."

"Hmm."

"Hmm?"

"Hmm."

"Don't you dare say you'd just shrug and smile, and everything would be alright. Some of us, meaning me, aren't used to living a public life. It's bad enough I had to call my parents, brothers, and closest friends and explain to them that the article wasn't what it looked like."

"How did that go?"

Her forehead creases and she gives me a look that says she doesn't want to talk about it. I shut it and let her give me the last couple of directions to the park. It's tiny and surrounded by a sea of average houses, with a play structure on one end and a few towering trees on the other. Clearly, it's been here for some time, based on the estimated age of those trees.

"Well, this is it. Probably not the kind you're used to, but then again, I'm sure nothing about this place is."

I somehow get the idea that Emily isn't talking about the park, the houses, or anything to do with the city. She's subtly talking about herself because she knows what kind of women I dated in the past, which is also searchable on the internet.

Growing up in a famous family, I just got used to constantly having a life that people could search up, comment on, and pick apart if they chose. That was just how it went. It's very hard to carve out a private bubble for yourself when you live in the public eye. I got used to living that way since I've done it from birth. This is truly the first time it all cuts straight down to a hollow pit inside me that I didn't even really know was there.

I want to say something sweet and profound, like tell Emily she's the most beautiful woman I've ever met, which she is, tell her she's brilliant, because of course, she is, tell her she's entirely captivating, unexpected, funny, tough, that she's completely unique, which is perfect since no one has the courage to live that way, and all that I know from just the past few days I've spent with her, but she jumps out of the car and slams the door in my face before I can get a word out.

I get out more slowly. My stomach hurts, and it's not from the tacos. My chest hurts, too, in an unfamiliar way.

I catch up to Emily, but my tongue is still glued to the inside of my mouth. The words churning through me are far worse than the gas pains I struggled with during the movie, and well, believe me, gas pains are nothing to scoff at. Especially when they threaten to let loose with a big rip in front of a packed theater. The action and suspenseful music would not have covered up the sound.

There's a little walking path we stick to. The park is pretty much big enough for a five-minute jaunt in either direction, so I know I don't have a lot of time before we reach the end and turn around to head back toward the car.

"Emily—"

"Asher—"

She turns to me at the same time as I turn to her, and our names come out in unison. However, before I can say anything, she's already speaking, her words tumbling out.

"I know I'm not, well, the kind of woman you usually date. I know I'm not tall, and I'm not exceptionally pretty. I'm not even that smart. I mean, I have two degrees, but neither of them involves having some kind of designation behind my name. I'm not famous, I've also hardly ever left St. Louis, and I have a regular life. A boring life. I'm actually so...so defunct that my last boyfriend, well, you know what he did, and—"

I can't stand to hear the nonsense she's saying. She's saying these things about herself though I know she can't possibly believe them. It's like she's making apologies to me for being who she is when everything about her is perfect, and even if it's not, she doesn't have to apologize for any of it.

I know there are zero words she's going to listen to at this point. I also know her eyes are huge and enchanting, her lips are parted at just the perfect angle, the sun is setting behind us, streaking the sky with a bunch of lovely colors, the park is peaceful and quiet, and there's an undercurrent of something inexplicable in the air. It might be the smell of the trees or some random exhaust fumes, but it sure as heck isn't taco gas. Whatever it is, it feels right, and I just go for it.

I cut her off mid-sentence by gently cupping her face, lowering mine, and claiming her mouth. At the first taste of her lips, my whole body erupts in flames. The fire is similar to the first time she kissed me, but this time, I'm not taken off guard. This is intentional. Goosebumps prickle the skin of my arms, and all the fine hairs there stand on end. Something else stands on end too, but I make sure to angle the lower half of my body away from her.

She makes a noise at the back of her throat, which I swallow. Her lips are warm and alive against mine even though she doesn't respond to the kiss. I happen to have a thing for strawberries, which is exactly what she tastes like. Sweet. A delicious explosion that tantalizes my tongue even though I haven't made good use of it yet. Her hands come up and press against my chest, and my thin t-shirt stands no chance of keeping out the heat of her touch. Now it's me that's making a noise.

"I can't!" Emily rips away, and she backs up a few feet, her chest heaving. "I mean, *we* can't! It's...that's not in the rules!"

I'm aware someone could be watching us right now, and I think she is too, so I step closer, shielding her from view. It's not hard because I'm just about twice her size. I lean in like we're having an intimate moment again and set my hand on her arm. She doesn't pull away. I'm not sure it's entirely because of how it's supposed to look. The expression on her face and the way her eyes dance with twin flames kind of makes me believe she doesn't have any desire to put distance between us. My heart starts pounding doubly as hard as it should.

I don't understand how a simple kiss can be so unnerving. For both of us.

"I'm sorry." I do mean it, although I'm not apologizing for the kiss. Rather, I'm sorry for the wall I've just put up between us. Emily might be standing close to me, but on

Mr. Charming (Not)

the inside, she's sprinting away like there's a pack of mutant bunnies chasing her.

Emily touches her lips gingerly like they're stinging. I get it. My lips are tingling like crazy too, and I feel like I've just put them in a bug zapper.

"Okay," she breathes shakily. "But that can't happen again."

"I know."

"Why did you..."

"Because you were going on and on about these flaws you seem to think you have, and I knew you wouldn't stop, and I wanted you to stop."

"So it was just that? Just a distraction?"

"No. I *wanted* to kiss you."

"Christ," she mutters. "You should have lied and said it was just to get me to be quiet. It would be easier."

"I'm sorry. It was to get you to be quiet. That's all."

She huffs. "But now I know the truth."

"We could walk again—around the park. And pretend like it never happened. You could tell me about your brothers, what growing up was like, and I could pretend you don't already know everything about me."

"I don't already know. I...I did look you up when I found out your grandma had bought us out, but I didn't do any psychotic research or anything. Just some regular research. I just wanted to know what was going to happen to our company. That was it."

"And since then, you haven't looked into me in more detail?"

"No." She pulls away, nervous now. She gnaws on her bottom lip, then sucks it into her mouth to ease the sting. Looking at it, I'd like to run my tongue there and find out all over again how sweet she tastes. The urge is stronger than I'd like to admit, so I move away an extra couple of inches to give us some space. We start walking again, at a snail's pace. "I know what your net worth is, where you were living before, and um...unfortunately, I know a bit about your dating history because that's easier to find than anything else, but that's it. I've been too busy lately trying to explain to the people closest to me what the heck I'm doing to actually do any creepy style research. So, why don't you go first? Tell me about what it was like growing up rich and famous and all. I really can't imagine. Even if I knew the details, reading about someone isn't everything. And I'm sure you had the most interesting life."

"You can say that." My tone is as strangled as I feel.

We start walking at a snail pace on the walking path, side by side. My hand is only inches from Emily's, and my fingers physically ache to reach out and close that gap, to wrap themselves around hers and hold them securely and protectively. It's a big deal to me because I can't remember the last time I even thought about hand-holding as exciting. Probably when I was thirteen.

"Oh. One of those. I see," Emily says, her voice thick with compassion. "I guess everyone wants to be rich, but no one ever thinks about how people who are born into it probably just want to be treated normally."

"I'm sure some of them like being rich and don't want to be treated normally at all. They like the perks. Honestly, I liked a lot of my childhood. My teenage years too. I got to go places all over the world, and I saw things that most people would give anything to experience. I liked having a famous granny, but there was a downside to it too. I've always grown up with the publicity, or whatever you want to call it—living a public life. It's hard to try and figure out what privacy means when I got so used to never having it.

My mom...well, I don't even know where to start. I love her, but she was wild. My granny has this saying about us putting her in an early grave. She's always lectured both of us with it, but maybe we both deserve it. My mom would be one of those people who likes all the money and fame, even if she didn't earn it. She was always raised with it too. I actually...I don't know who my father is, and she doesn't know either. That kind of wild."

Emily stops abruptly.

Yeah, I kind of just dropped that in the middle of nowhere. I haven't told anyone that before, and now it just came rolling out, as natural as can be.

"Jesus." I rake my hand through my hair and give her a sheepish grin. "Sorry. That was a little too weighty for a nice walk in the park."

"No. No, it's fine. I can't imagine growing up like that. I was raised too normally. Average middle class. That was our family. My brothers are both older, and they gave me hell. It was more than just the farting as they liked to be obnoxiously protective. I never even had a kiss until I was eighteen, at which time, they'd both gone off to college and weren't around to scare away potential boyfriends. Not that there were many lining up at the door."

"I can't believe that's true."

"It was."

"Because they didn't know how to ask. Beautiful women are always hard to talk to."

Emily snorts and rolls her eyes. "Yeah, right. Anyway, we did the normal family stuff—camping in the summer, skiing in the winter, that kind of thing. We're very boring. And we all went to college."

"You love classic literature."

"Yes." She laughs nervously, and I curse myself for

reminding her that I basically creeped her out hard with the background check. Because I have the power to do it. She finishes gently, though, without getting annoyed about my prying. "Yes, I do."

"I actually read a lot. You wouldn't think so because that kind of thing never makes magazine headlines. I've also been to lots of plays, shows, and musicals. All of that."

"Really? I would love to go to..." she trails off, realizing her error, and of course, I have to leap all over it.

"Yes! That's it. I'll find something, and I'll take you."

I have a private jet ride over to somewhere in Europe in mind. I'd buy out the whole house, and it would be just us. We'd watch a performance put on just for two people. Then we'd go to a five-star restaurant somewhere and end the night in a hotel suite.

Except I can't do any of that because Emily isn't really my girlfriend. As much as another woman might like it and has liked it because I've done all that before, I have the feeling Emily wouldn't enjoy it even if we really were dating. She'd protest that it was too extravagant, too much, and too not her. She'd probably tell me the money could be put to better use. I bet she's going to use the money I'm giving her for this for home repairs, or she'll give it to her parents for their mortgage or something because she's a good person, and of course, she'd think about others or something practical before treating herself.

"You have the strangest look right now. Are the tacos fighting back again?"

I exhale loudly, wiping the images of Emily in a hotel suite wearing nothing but my shirt, or maybe absolutely nothing, away. "Nope. I guess it's just what I look like when I'm thinking."

She lets out a loud bark of laughter. "Oh god. That's

frightening. Or not frightening, but you know. Sorry, that's rude. Just forget that."

We're nearly at the end of the park again, and I realize I've told her almost nothing, and yet somehow, I've told her everything.

"You know, I had a really good time actually," Emily says when we're back in the car.

"Like you might want to do it again?"

"Ha." She mimics laughter. "You wish. But I guess I'm going to be forced to, aren't I?"

"Forced is such a harsh word."

"Blackmailed?"

"Better."

"Persuaded by money and what you think is a charming smile?"

"Hey! What's wrong with my smile?"

"Nothing." Emily pauses. "Next date, we should go for tacos."

"Very funny." I use a tone drenched in dryness and then start the car.

Emily, at least, is entertained by this, and for some reason, it makes me happy. "Followed up by a show?" she suggests, all innocent, but I can tell she's barely clamping down on the riotous laughter.

"A show, we can do. I'll find something special."

"Why does that sound terrifying?"

"Terrifying? No. It sounds wonderful. Just trust me." She feigns more terror at that prospect.

"Let me guess," she cuts in before I can add anything convincing onto the end of a statement about trust when I've paid her to date me even though she barely knows me, screwed up her brand new table, and then ruined a movie with flatulence. "If the trusting thing doesn't work, I should just smile and shrug."

"Now you're catching on."

"Good lord." She shakes her head at me, but there is indeed a hint of a smile there.

That's a start. Now I just have to teach her how to give a proper—*I don't give two shats about the world and all its nonsense*—shrug.

10

EMILY

*H*ow does one exactly barge into one's boss's office and demand the money he owes her because a certain situation has arisen? I suppose dripping wet after being caught in a straight-up downpour from hell on one's way to work is how.

I burst through the open door of Asher's palatial office. Seriously, I wasn't even aware this place had an office this size. I shut the door behind me, push my soaking wet strands of red hair out of my eyes, and barely refrain from shaking out my wet clothes like a sopping wet mutt. The only difference between a dog and me right now is that dogs generally like to be wet and muddy. Me, on the other hand, not so much. It doesn't help that as I was running from the parking lot four blocks over, various cars passed me, spraying muddy water all over me more than once.

"Emily!" Asher jumps out of his desk chair and walks over in a few purposeful strides.

As usual, he's the picture of power and masculine grace. Dark hair neatly combed, white shirt pressed just so, pants probably pressed though not with those strange creases of yesteryear, and expensive leather shoes all polished right up.

I doubt he even knows what fair trade fashion is even though he owns this place.

His eyes start at my toes and do a slow, heated perusal over my sorry state. His pupils grow a shade or two larger, and his eyes stop at my chest, then flare. I glance down frantically, then let out a screech and fold my arms over my chest. Not only did I make the absolute shittiest choice and wear a white blouse, but I also wore a white bra. Not the pushup, super padded kind either. My nipples are practically poking through both clothing items, and even if they aren't on full display, they're certainly perky enough to get some notice.

Asher's notice.

His eyes jerk up, and he actually has the decency to look half apologetic. A strange flare of heat erupts in my belly just because he noticed my obvious nipples. Seriously, how desperate can I be that I'd feel semi-delighted about that? My body warms to the point where I'm shocked my soaking wet clothing doesn't start steaming.

"You should go home and change. Take the morning off. You can't sit in wet clothes all day."

"I was planning on going straight into the washroom and using the hand dryer on myself. I think that should do the trick."

"Are you serious?"

"No. I was planning on dripping at my desk until things dried out on their own. I'm tough like that."

"So tough that you wouldn't mind catching pneumonia since the AC is still on even though it's not overly nice out?"

I'm distracted, and it takes me a minute to tear my eyes

Mr. Charming (Not)

away from Asher and get myself back together. Which basically involves telling myself that I was not just appreciating him in his fine, masculine glory and swiping my sodden hair off my forehead so I can see. Not that I'm going to be using it to take note of Asher. Oh no. I've come with a purpose, and I need to make it known. I clear my throat. Loudly. Then I clear it again as Asher watches me with undisguised amusement. Clearly, I'm making his morning.

"I noticed the men showed up to work on my fence this morning. They were sitting in trucks with their company logo on the side, probably waiting for the rain to let up. Thank you for keeping that part of the bargain. And for uh...settling it out with the neighbors. I don't know what the lawyer said, but they came over last night and assured me that if I rebuilt the fence all the way around, which would include the length our properties share, they'd be more than happy with that."

Asher nods, but that's all I get. I'm losing my conviction here, so I know I have to keep going. There's an increasing pressure in my chest that makes me feel like an overblown balloon about to burst. I know this is going to be humiliating, but I have to do this.

"It's been quite a few days since you first came over with your proposition. Two days since our, erm, date in the park."

My pulse spikes just thinking about that kiss which I refused to participate. At least my lips didn't participate, but the rest of me was doing an internal party, the likes of which I've never felt before. Did I say party? I meant riot. Having your va-jay go rogue on you is not fun at all. I'm starting to think I might not be the only double agent around here. Maybe my lady bits are playing both sides as well.

Asher waits patiently for me to spill whatever I barged in here to announce. I think he knows what's coming as his eyes remain steadfastly locked with mine now. They don't dip down to my chest even once, where my arms are still firmly crossed over. I realize, all of a sudden, with the worst kind of panic, what it means. I glance down and realize I'm pushing my breasts up like two lush, round peaches. And my skirt is currently so wet that it's probably outlining my behind like the same ripe fruit.

Bloody bananas, I should not have come in here like this. Or anywhere.

Perhaps I should have called in to explain that I needed to go home and change. That would have been the smart thing to do. And grab a freaking umbrella along the way. No, instead, I marched in here like a drowned hussy.

Whatever. I'm here, and I'm ready to make my demands.

I can't make them out to the mysterious grandmother who appears and disappears like a pink-haired fairy godmother—a bribing godmother who doesn't grant wishes and who promises funds but doesn't deliver.

I lower my voice, unclench my arms a little, and decide that my humiliation is already about as bad as it can get. Asking for money isn't going to make it worse.

"Anyway, I was saying it's been quite a few days since we decided to…well, you know. Date. My brother called me last night, and he freaking lost his job. He got fired because he took too many sick days, but his wife is actually pregnant. She's seven months along, and had a couple of complications. She's had to have a lot of doctor appointments, and she's scared. I'm not going to get into it, but they need the money. My sister-in-law has health insurance through her work, and they won't drop her just because

Mr. Charming (Not)

she's pregnant and is having an extremely rough go at it. They're a good place, unlike my brother's work. Anyway, one salary, with a baby on the way and my sister-in-law having to take maternity leave, is going to be really tight for them. And I don't want them to lose their house. Melody doesn't need all this worry right now as it's not good for her or the baby. Anyway, I'm not trying to give you some sob story. I was just wondering if it would be possible to…to get the money you told me you'd pay me?"

I wish I could ask the granny for her twenty grand part of the deal, but of course, Asher doesn't know anything about that. I can't ask him to please phone her up for me and *get me my money*, even if it is in a nice way and kind tones. I'm not a threatening kind of person, even when I'm desperate. And I'm still debating whether I should be taking anything more considering Asher is already paying me so much already.

"Thank you for the fence. And the neighbors. And the table. And the movie the other night. You've paid for everything, and I feel a little bit like a leech, and now I'm worse because I'm leeching onto you, but kind of for what you already promised, and I'm not trying to be threatening or take it for granted that—"

"How much do you need?" Asher cuts in.

I cut myself off and gulp audibly. "What do you mean?" I'm so shocked that I drop my arms down to my sides, leaving my perky nipples unattended. "Just what you said. The twenty thousand."

"I'm asking you how much you actually need. For your brother."

Holy smokies. This guy is for real. There's genuine concern flashing in his eyes, which are the color of the sky right before all those nasty clouds gathered up and let loose on me this morning. My stomach drops the same way it did the first time one of those passing cars soaked me. I was frigid, sopping, filthy, and shocked that no one even bothered to slow down or care that they'd just deposited a tidal wave of nasty street water onto a pedestrian already struggling.

This morning kind of made me feel like there was no hope for humanity but now Asher's standing there, asking me how much money I need. Or rather, how much Sam and Melody need. He looks legit and not at all like he's going to ask me, then laugh in my face and tell me he was kidding about everything, including the twenty grand.

"I...I...I..." Apparently, my I's are in order because it's all I can stammer out. "I...don't know. It will probably take Sam a good few months to find another job, and their mortgage is probably around fifteen hundred a month. They have car payments, bills, the stuff for the baby to buy, groceries, and whatnot. But I really can't say. I was going to give them the money to help them out, so I hadn't run a total in my head."

Actually, that's exactly what I'd done. I'd come in here to ask if Asher would consider giving me an advance on my paycheck so I could give it to my brother.

"How about I double my offer?"

I gape at him while warning bells sound in my head. "With what kind of strings attached?"

"None. Same rules."

"Except you broke one already."

He legitly does look sorry—kind of. I feel sorry, too, though not really. Both times I've kissed Asher have been, oh, I don't know. Life. Freaking. Changing. How can I be sorry about that?

"I'll have it in your account within the hour if you give

me your information. I actually asked you for it before, but you hadn't given it to me, so I thought you weren't in a rush."

I realize he's right. I was the one holding out. I'd forgotten all about giving him my banking info. I guess, somewhere in the middle of trying to keep my life from going to total shit and then trying to pick up the pieces and hold what I had left together—namely my job—while explaining to my friends and family that I was doing my new boss a solid by pretending to be his girlfriend for a few weeks while giving them no more details than that, I must have forgotten.

Maybe I can look up his granny and give her the same information. She has to have some kind of a number I could reach her at. Or an assistant I could leave a message with.

"Are you...really? You would do that? I'm not trying...I was going to ask for an advance. I wasn't trying to come in here and beg money off of you."

"I know."

"But I feel like...I feel like...I don't even know."

"I hope it's something about a show and dinner and maybe a walk in a larger park, hopefully, tomorrow night. Because I have good tickets, and it also happens to be opera. I thought you might like it. Sadly, there were no plays featuring classical literature at the moment."

"The opera?" My head is turning into a tornado. "I've never been."

"But you'd like to?"

"I...yes. Of course. Who wouldn't?"

"Do you think your mom would like it?"

"My...my mom?" Now I feel like I'm lost in a fog. What does my mom have to do with it?

"Yes. Your mom."

Do not answer that. It's a trap. It has to be a trap. "I suppose she would." *Damn it.*

"Great. I bought two extra tickets in case your dad could be convinced to go as well. You'll ask them?"

Okay, this is seriously a trap. It has to be. He's trying to win my parents over. Or something. He knows they know this isn't real. But he still got them tickets? What could he possibly want from me? I'm not rich, and I'm probably not that great in bed either. I'm certainly no catch when he could have any woman he desires. And he's my boss. It's not like I can even lord that over him. He has me in every single way, and he knows it, but he's doing nothing to hurt me with any of that.

So I'm confused. Very confused.

What's his end goal here? He has to have one. Everyone has one.

"Tomorrow," Asher says calmly. "At seven. It's fine if they don't want to come. You can leave the decision up to them."

"I...thank you," I mutter. It's not an appropriate response, but I'm not sure what exactly there is to say. "I'm going to go home and change now." I wince. Yeah, because that's any better.

Asher nods. "I thought you might. And just so you know, I'm very excited for tomorrow for our date but not really a date night."

He lets me see myself out of his office.

11

EMILY

Halfway through the opera, Asher has my parents eating out of the palm of his freaking hand. They love my boyfriend, who's technically not my boyfriend. Maybe that's why they love him. My dad doesn't have to be all wary and protective, and my mom doesn't have to do any assessing. They can just sit back in the seats right beside me and enjoy the opera.

I have to admit I have tears in my eyes for more than one reason. The opera is incredible, and I can't believe I've never been before. The tickets, especially where we're sitting, second row in the middle, probably cost a fortune. Regular tickets probably cost a lot too. The talent, the story, the costumes, the way the stage is set up, complete with the lighting, it's all like being in a dream.

You know what else feels like being in a dream and causing my eyes to want to water?

The fact that this morning, when I woke up, there wasn't just twenty grand in my bank account. There was fifty—one single transaction. Asher Paris deposited fifty thousand dollars into my account! How it's possible to even do a transfer that large, I have no idea. Maybe for him, his online banking limits are a little different from my own. If someone else does his banking, perhaps they're used to moving huge sums of money around. When I randomly checked it, I was not prepared to see all those zeroes at the end. I mean, normally, there are zeroes, but they aren't in the right column.

I have no idea how I feel about that.

I now have enough money to help Sam and Melody and get my parents the kitchen renovation their house badly needs. They're still in the same home we grew up in, and the kitchen hasn't been updated since before I was born. My mom's appliances are so ancient that they barely work. I could even get a crew in there to make it happen for them since I know they can't do it themselves.

As soon as I saw the money, I had one thought. Is Asher Paris trying to buy me? That's the only thing I could figure. But then, after thinking about it for a large part of the day when I should have been working, I also thought that maybe he's just trying to be nice.

Or maybe he's a snake in the grass waiting to strike, and there's something I have that I have no idea I have, but he wants it. It could be that he's just toying with me. Maybe he gets off on stuff like this—power trips. Having someone owe him, or having someone in his debt.

But I don't think so. There wasn't, and isn't, anything in his demeanor tonight or from before that would suggest he has some underlying motive. In fact, he's sitting beside me like a perfect gentleman. Clad in a black suit that made my mouth water like he was a bag of salt and vinegar chips because yes, he looks that good.

After the opera is over, we see my parents off into their cab. Asher picked me up, and I was surprised until I realized that, of course, he was confident in doing valet parking. There's a huge lineup of people waiting for that same service right now. We're standing in the middle of the sidewalk, so I take a step back to get out of the way of the swirling crowds.

The city is nicely illuminated at night, so it doesn't truly feel dark. The summer makes it possible to fully enjoy the night because even in a black dress that falls just to my knees and a thin cardigan, I'm at the perfect temperature.

I know I shouldn't start a conversation this way, but I can't help being blunt. I turn to Asher—who looks just as dazzling right now in that black suit as he did at the start of the evening when I first climbed into his car and saw him—and blurt out the very thing that's been on my mind all day.

"What exactly is it that you want from me?" It comes out as a whisper, but not a harsh one. I just want to know.

"I knew you'd be angry," Asher says flatly. "That's why I didn't tell you before I did it."

"I want to return it." I mean, I do, but I also don't. But I do. Because I have to. I can't freaking keep fifty grand, even if I wouldn't be keeping it for myself.

Asher shakes his head. "No." A strand of dark hair comes loose and drapes over his forehead, and his eyes seem to shine in the dark, reflecting the lights around us. They're a deeper blue than I've ever seen them before. "It's already done. I won't hold it over you if that's what you're worried about. I'm not trying to buy you or embarrass you. I'm just trying to help."

"Help?" I gasp. "That's a heck of a lot of help. No one gives help like that without expecting something in return."

"Maybe I do."

I go with a different tactic. A very true one. "There are other people who need it more than I do."

"I know that. We actually…well, my granny mostly, has many charities she supports. So we do that too. Regularly."

I shift from foot to foot. My heels are sky-high. I don't normally wear them, so they're pinching my toes while simultaneously making the balls of my feet burn with a wicked fire. "There are still more people out there who could be helped."

"I know. But they're not my girlfriend."

"Neither am I." There hasn't been a single story about us since that kissing incident, and I haven't seen any photographers following us around. Once they found out I was so normal, did they just give up? Or are they brooding nearby, just waiting for a stellar moment to capture?

Asher ignores that. "I don't want you to worry, so stop stressing." He steps forward and points at the line. "Looks nearly empty. Let's go."

My feet hurt too much for me to protest, so I just go along. I have the strange feeling that if I told Asher about how painful the heels were, he'd tell me to take them off and go without. Which I would never do on a city street, so then he'd probably sweep me up into those massive, burly arms of his and carry me to the car. That idea should not be alluring, and I should not want to feel his muscles straining under his suit. I should not want to feel his skin brush up against mine, feel his warm breath on my cheek or the crown of my head, or hear his heartbeat slamming against my ribs. Except, frick. Now my nipples are trying to shred my dress, and it's the most expensive one I own. And also, my feet aren't the only things that are aching and throbbing now.

The car comes around for us, and Asher holds my door.

Mr. Charming (Not)

I slip in, and he gets behind the wheel right after. He drives with easy confidence like he actually enjoys it. I have to confess that I hate driving, and doing it at night is even worse. But being a passenger, though? The car is the perfect temperature, and it's late, after a long day. I find myself melting into my seat, just enjoying the lights and scenery as we pass.

Soon, we're at my house before I'm truly ready to be, which is jarring. Asher pulls up in the driveway behind my car and kills the engine.

"Can I walk you to your door?" As if there are dangers lurking in every shadow and around every corner.

"I..." Can I end the evening just like this? Can I send him off thinking I'm incredibly ungrateful for this wonderful night out and the insane amount of money he gave me?

No. That would be wrong in every way.

My parents taught me manners, and they'd both give me a lecture right now if I just got out of the car and shut the door in Asher's face. Besides, he'd still be at work on Monday. And every day after. It's not like I wouldn't have to face him sometime.

"Why don't you come in? For a drink?" That sounds like an invitation to do other things because a drink is never just a drink, and a drink usually means alcohol, though I currently have none of that in stock. "Um...of water. Or milk. Or juice. Tea? Something?"

Asher grins easily, and I watch his lips, mesmerized like a total ninny. "I'll take a glass of the something."

I let us in, and Asher goes right to the couch in the living room and takes a seat, throwing one arm out over the backs of the cushions.

"Don't make yourself at home or anything." I'm just

teasing, and he knows it. I guess it might be my poor attempt at flirting, but god, I'm out of practice. And really? Am I really flirting? Because if I was just flirting, it needs to stop in the worst way.

I'm not sure what counts as something, but I figure water is a safe bet since everyone probably likes water. After I pour two glasses and down one, I figure maybe Asher doesn't drink tap water. Unfortunately, it's all I have, so I bring it into the living room and set it down on the coffee table.

"If that something isn't to your liking, I can get you something else."

"Sounds good." He tips the glass to his lips, and as he swallows back the contents in two big gulps, his Adam's apple bobs. "Ahhh. Nope. That something was great."

I guess we were both parched.

I take the loveseat across the way and try not to stare. Asher, on the other hand, doesn't have any qualms about eyeing me openly and with interest. He maintains eye contact, though, and he doesn't let his gaze stray over me, so I'm not sure why I suddenly feel like I've just gone up in flames the same way the fence in the backyard met an untimely end.

"I should apologize…" I guess that's the best way to start what I'm sure is going to be a long ramble. "For making it seem like I wasn't grateful for what you gave me."

"I know you weren't ungrateful. You just had to put up a fight because it's who you are, and I knew you'd be both angry and uncomfortable when you found out. It's me who should apologize. I should have had more tact."

It takes me a second, but when I finally let out a little laugh, it turns into a full-on belly-busting kind. "Oh goodness..." I pant. "I'm apologizing for receiving it, and you're apologizing for giving it. That's quite a pair."

Asher grins at me and seemingly decides that I'm open for awkward conversation because his next question would blow my socks off if I were wearing any. "It was nice meeting your parents tonight. When do I get the pleasure of meeting some of your friends?"

"Oh no! We are *not* doing that. My parents loved you, by the way. The next time I see them, they are no doubt going to harass me about dating you for real. My friends would probably love you too. But I don't have that many. No, that sounds bad. I know lots of people, but my close friends are the ones I'm talking about."

I'm embarrassed to admit that I'm a bit of a workaholic, and life is just kind of busy the rest of the time. Not that I really admitted it, at least not out loud, but *I* know it. I'm also pretty ashamed to be sitting here, just thinking about that now, about how I got so caught up with all the silly things that don't even mean anything that I haven't talked to some of my friends in ages. Also, a lot of my friends didn't really like Byron, and I made the classic mistake of being loyal to him and not to them.

"What's wrong with me meeting them then?"

If Asher can change the subject and bounce around, then so can I. "Thank you for taking me out tonight. It's the first thing I've done in a long time that was fun. Other than the other night. That was pretty fun too."

Asher's right brow arches and the corner of his mouth draws up with it. "Yeah? Why not invite your friends next time?"

Great. So we're back to this. "I don't know..."

"Do you have a best friend?"

"No. I never actually had one, even growing up." I

remember how much that used to bother me until I became old enough to realize that having any number of people who care about you is a great thing. They don't have to have the label of bestie to be in your corner and be there when you need them.

"Neither did I. The way I was raised made that kind of impossible."

"That's shitty."

"We moved a lot and bounced around all over the place. You can imagine the rest. Anyway, I have lots of friends now. Kind of, sort of, whatever. It's on the bucket list—make a best friend."

I open my mouth, slam it shut, then open it again. "That's probably not a bad item to add to a bucket list. Not bad at all."

Asher points at the glass on the table. "I wouldn't mind a refill if that's okay."

I was thinking the same thing, though I'm not sure if it was the wine during the intermission earlier, the half bag of potato chips I scarfed down for dinner because I was starved and had zero time to get ready for the opera after leaving work—no, chips are not my usual diet—or the flames that lick up my skin every single time I glance Asher's way. Feeling all hot and bothered could definitely dry a person out and leave them extra thirsty.

"Sure." I grab his glass and walk off to the kitchen.

I take some time in there, sipping at the glass I refilled for myself. I don't know why my body is a wreck, and my breathing is all gaspy and raspy. The rest of me feels gaspy and raspy too, but in actual fact, I do know why. It's Asher. Ten out of freaking ten Asher. It would be easier to dislike him if he was a totally self-centered, obnoxious jerk of a nob, but he's not. He's the kind of person who

Mr. Charming (Not)

takes my parents to the opera and gives me a massive bonus when he finds out my family needs help.

How could the women he's actually dated for real in the past let him slip away? Why let him go? Why not fight for someone like him? He seems, despite the fact that he has money, some sort of fame, power, and good looks—the whole deal really—well, *nice*.

I realize I've been in the kitchen forever, so I swallow thickly, take Asher's full glass, and head back to the living room.

Only to find him passed out on my couch. His head is thrown back against the pillows, his one arm still outstretched. His mouth is parted slightly, and he's snoring softly. It's more of a gentle buzz. Is that really snoring, or is it just heavy, even sleep breathing?

Holy pineapples, if I fell asleep like that, just straight passed out, I'd look repulsive, and I'd probably have drool dribbling down my chin. Maybe snot too? My eyes would likely be doing some creepy REM thing behind my lids. I wouldn't be doing the cute kind of snoring he's doing, that's for sure. I'd probably be more like sawing some freaking logs with the rustiest of chainsaws.

But Asher?

Even sleeping like that, he's beautiful. Totally. Freaking. Unblemished.

The glass of water ripples in my hand, and I gently set it down on the coffee table. I force myself to tear my eyes away because maybe he's just fake sleeping to see if I stare at him, and this is all some sort of game. I wait, studying the floor. After a few minutes, Asher doesn't wake up, so I think he really is asleep.

I dare another look at all that unguarded beauty. My breath catches and balls up in my throat. When I let it out, it sounds like an ungraceful belch of a chainsaw, and I'm awake.

I recall how I thought about Asher after walking out of the movie to find him. I thought about him as a person—not as someone above me, not as my boss, and not as this powerful billionaire with a granny who makes super amazing clothing for a living. I thought about him as a man who was complicated but also simple, someone who was just a person underneath all of it.

Right now, he's just a man who is tired enough to pass out on my couch, just like I sometimes do after a long day.

I should shake him awake and tell him it's time he gets going, but I just can't make myself do it. Instead, I grab the throw blanket off the loveseat and cover approximately three percent of his massive body with it. I have to lean in close to tuck the blanket over his shoulder, and as my finger accidentally brushes against his shirt collar, I watch his pulse thrumming there in his neck.

I should stop while I'm ahead because technically, that touch was an accident, but I just can't. He's truly dead asleep, so I brush the fingertip of my index finger over his forehead. I jerk back at the smoothness of his skin. It truly is like a baby's bottom. He's warm too. So warm.

I jerk back, and not just because my own internal warmth—meaning the flames that seem to be burning me to a charred crisp—is back. I know I'm getting more than a little touchy-feely creepy, and I need to stop.

But I can't.

I guess I'm going for the creep of the year award after all because I gently run my fingertip over his full bottom lip. The skin there is so soft. As soft as I knew it would be because I remember every single detail about his lips.

Maybe he wasn't sleeping after all, and I just failed this

test, or maybe he was sleeping, and my blatant perusal woke him. All of a sudden, his eyes slowly flicker open. I need to jerk back, but I'm frozen in place, leaning over him like a boogey man from the worst nightmare, my finger still on his bottom lip.

Asher doesn't smile, and he doesn't shrug. Instead, what he does do is part his lips, lean forward, and suckle my finger into his mouth.

And holy papayas, I finally think I know what it would mean to die a happy woman.

12

ASHER

"You could have done anything to me," I murmur against Emily's lips. It's a funny thing to say when you're kissing a person.

"What?" she pulls back and sets her hand on her tingling lips.

"Whipped cream and a feather, shaved off an eyebrow, scanned my fingerprint to whatever ends you choose..."

"That's ridiculous."

"You could have felt me up. I could have been violated in sleep."

Emily's eyes shut, and the red starts creeping up from her collarbones. "Oh my god," she breathes. "I didn't. Really."

"I know."

I grip her around the waist and gently pull her into my lap. I don't know if it's because I still have the element of surprise, but she doesn't fight me. I tip her mouth up and lean down, lingering on her lips. They meet, but barely, and electric sparks shoot up as if I've just been abducted like that poor cow or goat you always see in an alien ship beam.

Her lips are blazing hot—soft, pliable, and willing. With a moan, she turns into me, pressing the soft pillow of her breasts against my chest, wrapping an arm around my neck, and tangling my hair with her fingers. Her other hand grips my arm, and she squeezes hard like she wants to feel my skin through the fabric of my shirt.

Her lips part as she exhales, and when I taste her bottom lip with my tongue in a perusal that seems to happen in slow motion—and believe me, I have never been more excited for slo-mo in my life—she doesn't clamp up or bite down on my tongue. I've never had my tongue bitten by someone else, and it's an experience I'd rather not find out about.

Just like the two times I've kissed her before, it seems like some floodgates of something I've never experienced open up, and the sensations that flood me are completely brand new. It's like Emily is the first person I've ever kissed.

My entire body reacts. My chest tightens, my heart slams, my balls clench up, and I have no doubts that Emily can feel my pokey stick poking her.

Her mouth parts on a whimper, and I taste her fully, thrusting my tongue inside her mouth. Her tongue is waiting, stroking mine eagerly. She makes another sound in her throat, something that sounds like, *ermfh,* then *glarmph,* then more distinctly, *fuck it.*

Emily swivels around, straddling me. She then knocks me back on the couch, cups my face, and attacks my mouth, and I give in because who the heck wouldn't give in. I want this. I want her. I want to taste her, and I want to undress her and linger on every bit of her creamy, delicate skin.

She shifts her hips, and a blaze of white-hot heat writhes through me with the movement. She's wearing the dress from earlier this evening, and I can feel the hot heat of her center pressed up against the bulge in my pants. When she grinds against me, pressing down hard and moaning, I nearly burst right out of my pants. Or quite possibly burst in them. I feel terribly out of control, but instead of being humiliated by the strength of my desire, I'm even more excited.

Emily sinks her teeth into my lip and gently bites down on it. I nearly leap off the couch at the sensation. She presses me down, though, with all her tiny weight, which is half of my own or less, but right now, my body feels like it weighs a thousand pounds—in a good way. My head feels light, though—dizzy, strange, and absolutely wonderful.

I battle with Emily's mouth and her tongue in a kiss that makes everything around us hazy. It's just us, and I don't want to stop. God, *I want her*. It's not just about wanting her body, either. I want *her*. The real her. I want to see that too.

Alarms sound in what's left of the bits of my brain that can actually focus. Emily is different. Even that first kiss with her was different, though I don't know what it is. I don't know why the prospect of fake dating her was far more exciting than any real dating I've ever done, and I don't know why I can't stop thinking about her. She's probably the only woman I know who can casually talk about bad gas, but that's not what makes her unique. I can't figure it out, but I know that whatever it is about her is driving something in me that I've never let loose or given any consideration to before. Maybe not driving, but matching it, drawing it out. And it's utterly terrifying because it's hard

Mr. Charming (Not)

for me to admit there are bits of myself that I know nothing about.

All I know is there's an ache in my chest which could rival my balls, and I've never felt anything like it. The newness of it burns through me, but then Emily moves against me, pressing herself against my aching dick, her pert breasts pressing into my chest, her lips claiming mine, and I lose it—the ability to be rational and feel fear about what this could mean for me.

All I know is there isn't anything fake about what we're doing.

This is real. Our arousal, our bodies, the connection.

Suddenly, a sharp crack somewhere in the house breaks us apart. Emily leaps from my lap, but her legs get caught on the couch. She bites down on a scream, so all that comes out is an astonished gasp as she plunges backward over my knees. I quickly catch her flailing hands, such that she's hanging upside down, bent over backward.

"Oh my god." I carefully lean forward and set one hand on her neck while I take both her hands in my other hand and gently pull her up. "Are you okay?"

"Holy guacamole, that was the AC. It sometimes makes that noise. It's terrible. Like a freaking gun shot. I need to get it looked at as it scares the bejesus out of me every single time."

I can see the doubts swimming in her eyes, but when I lean in though, she doesn't pull away. And when our lips meet, there isn't any hesitance. I cup her waist and stand, lifting her easily and cradling her to me so that there isn't a repeat of the backward cartwheels. She cups my face between her warm palms and kisses me eagerly.

"Down the hall," she pants. "Stairs...bedroom is..."

The only word that registers with me is *bedroom*.

I stiffen, but only because I want to make sure Emily truly wants this, but she digs the heels of her bare feet into my ass and rasps against my lips, "Please. God. Now. Yes," wriggling against me again so that my brain malfunctions and I have zero control left.

I find the stairs and climb them. I even manage to take Emily's directions as she steers me silently with her foot pressing into my bottom because I've claimed her lips again. I find the bedroom too and push open the door. It looks bedroomy. Well, there's a bed, at any rate. And some dressers, nightstands, blinds at the two windows—just the regular.

There are a few pieces of clothing on the floor. But not enough. Not enough, because ours are still currently on. When I set Emily down on her bed, she whimpers, and her hands cling to the front of my shirt as she tries to tear it from my body. I start working the buttons undone, and she watches me intently. I watch her, too, as my fingers fly.

This isn't like my other experiences. This is...this is the first time in my life that I have a feeling in my gut that I'm going to give something away here. Something I didn't truly understand I had until now.

With an impatient grunt, Emily reaches up and frantically helps me with the rest of my buttons. Then, I shove the shirt away and lean down over her. She wraps her arms around my neck, her legs around my waist, and tugs so hard that my feet come straight off the floor. Luckily, I catch myself with an elbow and my lips—my lips on Emily's. Our mouths meet, and our tongues clash wildly, consuming each other. Emily strains against me. She wriggles, and her dress rides up. When she finds her spot, she grinds deliciously against me.

And I swear my entire life flashes before my eyes.

Mr. Charming (Not)

I guess that's what happens when all the blood rushes from every extremity in my body and ends up straight in my dick. It's quite dangerous, actually.

I guess there must be something left that my brain is running on, or maybe it's just autopilot because my hand moves, sweeping Emily's dress aside. I cup her breast, and she arches up and moans out something muffled against my lips.

I find delicate lace beneath the dress, and my balls clench up. They're probably three times more purple now than they were a second ago. I sweep my thumb under the lace and find Emily's nipple hard and perfect. Breaking the kiss, I lower my head and taste the sweet perfection of her nipple.

"Oh my god," Emily gasps as she threads her hand through my hair and pulls violently. "God, Asher, yes…"

I ply the straining bud, suckling it into my mouth and scraping it gently with my teeth. Emily thrashes beneath me. I don't think I've ever had this much joy of doing anything, and we're still dressed here. Kind of. I lick Emily's breast, straying from her nipple as I taste her all over. Her skin is sweet, with just a hint of salt, and I'm reminded of chocolate caramel sea salt fudge. I don't have a weakness for sweets, but I do have a weakness for that.

I need more. I need more of her on my tongue, in my mouth, so I leave her breasts and trail kisses down her dress—which is absolutely not tasty at all—until I reach her stomach, where the fabric is rucked up. I taste her skin again, licking, kissing, and grazing her with my teeth.

"Oh sweet heavens," Emily moans. "This is more satisfying than *anything*. Even axing that table and setting it on fire."

"I'll take that as a compliment."

Before long, my fingers find the soft silk of her black panties. They're warm with the heat of Emily's body and also completely soaked. I feel like weeping with joy at having the pleasure of touching her. "Can I taste you here?"

"Sweet tomatoes," she whimpers. "I...what if I'm not...I don't know. Perfect?"

I laugh at that, my shoulders shaking until I realize she's not just making a joke. "Are you serious?" I dip a finger under the soaked fabric, coat it in her arousal, and pop it into my mouth. I suck it clean, her spicy sweetness bursting over my tongue. My dick is hard enough that should the table magically reincarnate in the kitchen, I think Emily could use *me* as her weapon of choice to destroy it all over again.

"You're the most perfect thing I've ever tasted," I say huskily. This isn't just bedroom talk, sweet nothings, platitudes, or whatever people call it. It's a hundred percent true. "Tasting you is like tasting the nectar of the gods."

"Jesus," she says dryly. "Laying it on a little thick, aren't you?"

"Like water to a dying man."

"Oh my god. No."

"Like all the particles of some unknown magic aligning to create another universe that is completely flawless."

She giggles at this, and I grin. "You're ridiculous," she murmurs.

"And you, my dearest lady, are absolutely beautiful."

"My dearest lady? How medieval."

I slide off the bed and kneel on the rough carpet below. The stuff is very rough and thready. It's a good thing we have the bed because the floor wouldn't be an option. The rug burn would be unbelievable.

I lift Emily's knees, and her legs part for me, revealing

Mr. Charming (Not)

all that black silk. I gently peel those panties away, revealing my true prize—Emily, ready and so wet for me. I groan because it's indeed possible that I've entered some parallel universe of total, wondrous perfection.

Her hands grasp for my hair, but one misses, and she snags my ear like an angry school teacher. She giggles shyly. "Sorry," she whispers. "Oh my god, I'm not good at this."

"Not good? I beg to differ." I trail my hand along the inside of her thigh, and she shivers. "I think you're *very* good at this."

She giggles again, a nervous laugh like she doesn't believe me.

"I think you're far more wonderful than you even realize."

"Stop," she begs. "You're making me blush, and right now, I'm nervous enough."

"You're delicious, entirely intoxicating, irresistible, and the flame that lights the way in the darkest night."

"The flame that burns down my backyard and incinerates you," she protests dryly.

In reply, I run my hands up Emily's silky thighs, and her breath catches. I dip my head, kissing her smooth skin where my fingertips are splayed. Her skin breaks out in goosebumps, and I can feel the shiver that sweeps up her legs and rattles her entire body. I look up to see her staring at me, her eyes darker and wider than ever.

I move my hand, brushing a finger down her silky, hot center. She moans wildly. I replace my finger with my mouth. I use my tongue and my fingers, and Emily is instantly responsive. Her hips rise up, and she bucks into my touch.

"I think you are *very* good at this." I also think she's the most delicious thing I've ever tasted. She whimpers at my words, and when I taste her again, she's immediately responsive. Her hips thrust up, and when I stroke her with my finger, dancing around her entrance, teasing her there, she thrashes her head against the bed.

Her arousal coats my lips as she gets wetter, and I swirl my tongue through her, gathering it all up like a treasure. She *is* a treasure. *Emily.* I feel incredibly undeserving of being the one to touch her. This woman, who swept into my life in the most unexpected way, who dared to kiss a complete stranger, who claimed me with a single kiss, and who set all of this in motion.

I don't think I've ever felt anything quite this perfect. In fact, I don't just feel undeserving. I feel completely terrified of the new feelings. Things I haven't been able to block out since I met Emily. Things I've never felt before.

Emily's fingers pinch my ear again while her other hand tangles in my hair. She's gentle, even when I lick her from top to bottom. Then, I suck on her clit, saving it for last.

"Oh my... stars..." Emily pants. "It doesn't matter if I'm good at this. You're good at it. So good."

"I told you that you were perfection."

"Your tongue is perfection."

I smile before I use my tongue to worship her clit. I know what she needs, and even though I wanted to draw this out, I can feel her straining for release. I want to give it to her. That pleasure. That wonder. I tease her entrance while I swirl my tongue over her clit, then I push my finger in, filling her.

"Oh my god, Asher..." She writhes above me, her body taking over.

I can feel her straining, and when I thrust up into her

Mr. Charming (Not)

and suckle her clit hard, she shatters. Her fingers curl hard into my hair, and she nearly rips my ear off with the other hand. Her tight, slick passage squeezes around my finger as her clit pulses below my tongue. She pants and moans through her climax.

"Holy cheese and crackers," she cries. "Asher. More. Please. Don't freaking stop."

How could she have thought she wasn't good at this? She's the most beautiful goddess that was ever created. She's soaking wet, and I lap at her sweet juices, tasting her pleasure. She's so sweet and rich that my body aches with a ferocity I've never known. God, I want to be inside her. I also want this to be perfect for her, which involves letting her tell me what she wants. If she's not ready for that, then I'm ready to keep on doing whatever she commands I do.

Even if it's just to lay beside her and hold her all night.

Which is, uh, something I've never done before.

Yes, that's right. I'm one of those guys who doesn't do cuddling. Partly because it's never been asked of me before. Intimacy isn't exactly my specialty, but if it's what Emily wanted, I would happily give it to her. Actually, more than happily, which makes my chest ache worse than my balls at the moment.

Emily cups my face when I raise it. "Please, don't stop," she whispers thickly. She can't see me since the edge of the bed is hiding me from the waist down, but she can probably guess what's going on for me south of the border. "I'd like to...to...taste you if I could," she mumbles shyly.

"Taste me?" I grunt.

"Touch you...Is that alright? If I...if I enjoy you, I mean, I hope you'd enjoy it too."

I groan like a feral pumpkin bitten by a mangy werewolf at the thought of Emily doing anything to me.

Emily blinks at me. "I hope that's a yes. I mean, I know I'm probably not good at *that* either, but I'd—"

I have to wrap my fists tightly in the quilt on the bed to keep myself upright. Then, I cut the rest of her words off with a kiss that leaves both of us breathless. Emily thrusts her tongue into my mouth, tasting herself moaning, craving, and falling while I'm doing all of that too. Moaning. Craving. Falling.

"Oh yes," I assure her between pants. "It most definitely is a yes."

13

EMILY

I want to tug Asher up onto the bed, but I know I don't stand a chance lifting him. Duh. But he gets up and stands right in front of me. I sit up and take in his rugged beauty. Every single detail from those broad shoulders to his hard-cut abs is sheer perfection. Even his nipples and the tiny amount of dark hair around his naval are sheer awesomeness. I also love the corded veins that run the length of each bulging muscle.

I gulp hard and continue to gape in open admiration. I'm not shy about it at all, and neither is Asher. I have to say if he were staring at me, and I was semi-nude, I'd be just a *tad* self-conscious. I'm not all bulgy and cut like he is, though. I mean, the female version of it, whatever that might be. Lush and curvy? Busty? Big-bottomed? Jeez. I don't even know what is actually trendy right now.

Which is fine. Anyway, I'd really like for Asher to take off his pants, though I'm not sure how to ask without appearing very forward or slightly horribly desperate, so I scoot forward on the bed and reach out. I run my finger over the sheer delight that is his ridged stomach until I reach his pants. Wordlessly, I slip them open and undo the zipper. Suit pants are much easier to undo than jeans, thank goodness.

"I'd like these off," I whisper, giving voice to my desires even though I wasn't planning on it. I tug hard, but Asher's hands grasp mine.

"I wasn't sure how far you wanted to take this."

"As far as, uh, well…until it, yeah. As far as it goes and as much as it takes?"

"Which would be…"

"Um, I…I don't have a condom," I admit. I shyly drop my gaze to my hands, which are still surrounded by Asher's big ones.

"I do. But I want to make sure you're sure."

"Oh. Yes, I'm *very* sure."

"Alright." He lets my hands go and then sheds his pants and boxers himself.

My eyes nearly pop out of my head when I see his um… proud flagstaff proudly flying at full mast. Apparently, all of Asher is big. And hard. Very. Hard.

I want to touch him. I want to run my hand down the length of him, from the swollen tip right to the base. I want to learn what he likes, and I want to let him show me. I'd be a fast learner. I feel very throbby and empty, so I'd like him to sate that ache, fill me up, and wow, what does that make me? Because I can't ever remember having urges like this in my life. Urges that are so desperate, if I can't fit us together soon, I'll probably go freaking insane.

"Would you like to drive?"

"Wh—"

"Never mind. How would you like to do this?" Asher asks as he bends down and produces a small foil packet from his pocket.

Mr. Charming (Not)

"That's a dangerous question," I mutter. "I'd like to do quite a few things to you."

"As long as I don't end up going the way of your table or fence, I'm up for it." He grins at me, which makes my hoo-ha curl in on itself and beg for mercy.

I have quite a few spur-of-the-moment fantasies I'd like to work through, but I realize there's probably a nice way to start out. Like a sort of way that's expected, though I'm not sure what it is. If I ask Asher to take me up against the wall, then in the shower, and on the living room couch, and if I say I want the table assembled just so we can break it all over again, he might say he's out of condoms.

Although, thinking about doing something like that starts a pronounced ache in my nether regions, the likes of which I've never felt before. I want him, and I want him badly. I need him inside me.

"The wall," I whisper, because why not start out ultra-dirty. I might as well shock him first, which I can see I have because one dark brow curls toward the ceiling.

"The wall?" he echoes.

I leap off the bed and walk over to the big empty space between the dresser, the wall, and the far window. I turn slowly, putting my hands against the cool surface.

"Lord above," Asher grunts. "You realize that...that almost ensures you won't receive your full dues. I mean pleasure. That...that it might be over before you expect."

I have no idea what he's talking about, but then suddenly, it clicks. Oh. Is he really saying what I think he's saying? It gives me a strange surge of something that makes my head feel all light and airy.

"I'm willing to chance it if you are." I just hope he has more than one wrapper wherever he pulled that one from. It's kind of late to be driving to the corner store with high hopes that they might have some, and I can't imagine how embarrassing it would be to walk into a place like that to buy condoms. What would people say anyway? *Oh, hi, I'd like a slice of pizza, two of those hot dogs, an extra-large soda, two scratch tickets for luck, and the largest box of condoms you have.*

Asher sucks in a breath, but I don't turn around, not even when I hear the packet rip open. And then he's there, right behind me, his huge body making me feel small, thrilling me, and making me feel extremely naughty because I still have my hands on the wall.

His hand trails up my thigh, pushing my dress up. My panties are long gone, and thankfully, they haven't magically reappeared like a freaking chastity belt from outer space.

"Lord, Em, if you only knew how much I want you…"

Well, his voice is throaty and delicious, and it makes me ache with the intensity of a hungry lion. I can feel moisture trickling down my thighs. "If you only knew how much I wanted you," I shoot back.

It's true. I haven't had sex in…let's just say a *very* long while. I can't say I've ever experienced an orgasm as good as what Asher gave me on the bed. I've never had mind-blowing sex, and I've been on this planet for three decades. I'm very, very ready.

I whimper when I feel Asher's cock, thick and swollen, throb against the inside of my thigh. His fingers brush over my center, then he palms himself, smearing my wetness over his length. I just about collapse, die, and have a spontaneous orgasm from that alone.

"Please, Asher," I beg. "I want you. I want to feel you. Now."

His finger brushes over my folds again, and this time,

he circles my clit, and I jerk violently. I let out a hiss when he leans against me, his heat scalding my back. I spread my legs and let Asher guide my bottom up. His cock presses up against my entrance, but then he stops. I'm sure he's going to ask me if I'm sure, so I wriggle my hips back into him so that he pushes inside. I don't want him to stop, and I know he doesn't want to stop, so I push back into him, taking him slowly, letting him fill me, stretch me, shock me.

He pushes in all the way, and I claw at the wall in response as I let out a long moan. I can't help myself. I writhe against Asher, taking him deeper. He pulls out halfway, dragging out the movement and pleasure, then thrusts back in hard. I ride with him, and we build a rhythm together. I can feel all the pleasure that's been locked away in me for my entire freaking life spiraling and tightening into something deep and unknown inside me.

Every thrust takes me to a magic land of dancing doughnuts and light beams. I know I'm close because I start to see purple llamas behind my closed eyes, but all of a sudden, the bottom of the world, the ocean, the sky, the ground, all of it drops out, and I'm floating, flying, and breaking. Shattering. Coming apart.

The climax hits me hard, rendering me totally speechless, but Asher feels it. He knows. He drives into me, thrusting hard, then buries himself deep inside me with a groan. His fingers clench around my hips while he shudders silently, and his heavy breathing is pretty much the only indication that he's gone somewhere else too. I wonder if he's making his way through the same magical land I just rocketed off to.

"Sprinkles," I blurt. I meant to finish it up with something else, but all that comes out of my mouth is that one word.

"Sprinkles," Asher agrees.

He pulls out, picks me up, and sets me on the bed. Then, he drags the comforter over me before disappearing. He has no problem finding the bathroom since I hear the light click on in the room just beside mine, but he's back a few minutes later. Surprisingly, he peels back the blankets and slips into bed beside me, taking me into his arms and tugging me up against his chest. His skin is cold and clammy from the air temperature mixed with his sweat, but I don't mind one bit. I'd like to be the one who warms him up, actually.

"Are you...it's kind of late. Are you thinking you'd like to stay the night? If you're not up for it, that's alright. Just don't pull a disappearing act halfway through because that would be more upsetting to me than if you just left now."

Asher's hand gently strokes my hair while his heart pounds fiercely right across from mine. "You'd be upset?"

"Hmm, I don't know if upset is the right word."

"I'll stay."

"You will?"

"Oh yes," he says darkly, and his sexy as sin voice gets my insides clenching and wanting again. "I'll stay."

14

EMILY

"Where's my grandson?"

"Arghflfhfhffhhhhhhh!" I wake to the sound of someone's sweet, soft voice. It's feminine, and it most definitely doesn't belong to Asher.

My eyes tear open, and somehow, my body reacts before my brain, and I turn myself into a projectile. One that lands straight on the floor. Thwump! I go down, dragging the sheet with me. Thank god, because I'm totally naked. My bare bottom hits the cold floor, and I let out another yelp. I scramble fast, hugging the sheet to me. Somehow, I manage to right myself, and I dive back under the quilt on the bed, pulling it all the way up to my chin.

Holy mother of grannies, it's a granny. A real live granny. With glowing pink hair in a glittery gold dress. She looks like a granny of fairy dreams, but nope, she's real. And she's really standing there, in my bedroom.

"What are you doing here?" With just my eyes, I glance frantically to the other side of the bed, so I don't give myself away, but nope. Asher isn't there. Why isn't he there?

"I knocked profusely on your door, but there was no answer. I tried the handle, and it was open, so I let myself in."

"You what?"

Who uses the word profusely to describe knocking? And why didn't I hear it? Oh right. Because I'm exhausted from the previous night's strenuous exercises. We did it multiple times. And um, I'm more than slightly sore. Which, under other circumstances, would be entirely wonderful, but right now, with a fire-breathing granny staring me down, it makes me feel guilty and flushed.

"That's right. I had to let myself in. I hope you appreciate the work I had to do to get here undercover."

"Ummm..."

Asher's granny has a matching gold clutch in her hand. Of course she does. Because it's okay to wear evening wear first thing in the morning if you're Julie Louise Paris.

"I'm going to ask you again. Where is my grandson?"

My eyes dart surreptitiously to the rumpled covers on the other side of the bed. How does she know he was here? Does she have paid spies watching us? I'd really like to know where Asher is too, but I'm not going to dignify her question with a response because it's private information. For me. And Asher. I'd like to know where he is too. I know he was here as of six this morning because I woke up for a few minutes, decided it was early as hell, turned over, and went back to sleep right next to him.

Asher's granny pulls a piece of paper out of her clutch and waves it around. A cheque, I realize. Jesus, did she seriously come here just to give me that? Nope. I bet she didn't. I can tell by the way her lips purse that she's not nearly done. This isn't just about a cheque at all. She could have easily deposited the money, but no. That cheque is

Mr. Charming (Not)

symbolic, and at the moment, it makes my stomach feel twisted and sour.

"I was paying you to fake date my grandson. To help him get settled. To show him that life is more than just… well…" She waves a hand over the bed and mussed sheets. Me. Over me. "I wasn't paying you to fall into bed and one night stand him. I know his charms are potent, but I expected more from you."

Ouch. Nothing like a granny tongue lashing first thing in the morning to stab me straight to the heart. And the gut. "That's not what happened," I blurt but then stop. No. I am not going there. I am not having this conversation.

Julie Louise Paris gives me that look. That granny look where one eyeball gets squinty and the other eye gets huge, and those lips purse more than ever. "I know," she whispers.

And I know she does. I can feel the heat crawling up my neck—heat of mortification, of anger, of…of wondering where the hell Asher is and how he could have left me to face his granny alone. God, if anything is potent, it's her.

"It's…it's your own fault," I stammer. "You blackmailed me into this in the first place." I swallow thickly. There really isn't any point in lying now. It's pretty obvious Asher's granny knows everything, which isn't at all creepy, and of course, that is thought with the heaviest sarcasm. "What we did, uh, was real. That wasn't…I wasn't…it's not a one-night stand."

Now Julie Louise Paris has this other granny look. The kind, sappy granny look that says she feels utterly sorry for me. The sort of look that says she knows her grandson a heck of a lot better than I do, and I'm being very stupid, though she wouldn't use the word stupid. Naïve is a better word. A nicer word.

My heart stops, and my stomach twists sickeningly again. I ball the quilt up in hands that are suddenly damp.

"I came to discuss something with you, but I can see that you get it. Now that I'm here, I'm going to surprise Asher. He'll want to have a family dinner, and he'll want to invite you so I can meet you. For appearances. You have to act surprised."

Right. Because the only reason Asher would ever invite me to dinner with his granny would be for show. Because this is what he does. This is how he dates women. Why did I think I was any different? Just because the lines between fake and um, well, you know, got crossed doesn't mean what Asher feels is real. It doesn't mean he's going to want to date me for real. And even if he did, his granny thinks that is one step below the faking it thing.

I don't want to feel like this. Used, chewed up, and just another conquest, as nasty as that word is. Is this what Asher does? I know he's dated a lot of women, but is this how he made all of them feel? That they were different? Special? Treasured?

Fuckstack, I am an IDIOT. I can't believe it took his granny ninjaing her way into my place to make me understand that.

"I'm tired of acting," I snap as the wounded ache in my chest turns into brutal anger. "I'm tired of all of it. I wish I could just up and move, but I was here first. It was my company before it was yours, and it was my city first."

Julie Louise Paris shakes her head like she's tired, and there is a hint of some sympathy in her expression now. "Maybe it was a terrible idea. All of this. Maybe I should ask Asher to move somewhere else."

We stare each other down with doubts, narrowed eyes, pain, confusion, hurt, wounded pride, more doubt, love on

Mr. Charming (Not)

her end, and probably some sad, pathetic, watered-down expression on mine.

"I like your hair," Asher's granny says out of freaking nowhere. "But your choice of attire sucks."

"I'm sorry?" Because currently, I'm not wearing anything but a sheet and a quilt.

"I looked through your closet before I woke you up."

Oh my good freaking unicorn sprinkles. She did not.

"It's all stuff from your company, thank you very much."

Julie Louise Paris just rolls her eyes. "I'll have something sent over for dinner. My treat." She bends, grabs the quilt at the end, and yanks it away. I yelp and pull the sheet up higher, but it's white and probably hides nothing at all. This lady might very well be not only a ninja but a crazy ninja—a crazy ninja granny.

"A size eight?"

"Y...yes." All the clothes in the closet are sized small, medium, and large, so it's a good guess. A really good guess. I'm starting to think Asher's granny has strange powers. Like X-ray granny vision.

"Good. I'll see to it."

Then, she turns and walks out. Just. Like. That. Like letting herself into someone else's house, inspecting their closet, waking them from a dead sleep, and giving them a lecture about life is no biggie.

I jump out of bed and throw on some clothes. Even they feel violated, now that I know Asher's granny went through my closet. I'm just pulling on a sweater over my tank when Asher appears in the bedroom doorway like a ghostly phantom. I didn't even hear the door open downstairs. What is it with the Paris family?

He's holding two paper coffee cups in his hands, and it's obvious where he was. So he didn't abandon me, didn't leave in the middle of the night, or steal away like he was ashamed and leave my door unlocked for just anyone to come in here and kill me. He was probably gone for all of twenty minutes, and his granny knew perfectly well that he'd left. She was probably watching the house all camped out, dressed in camo, with black paint smudged under her eyes.

Okay, I'm getting ahead of myself.

Before I can say anything, Asher gives me that beautiful Asher smile which I've become incredibly used to in a shockingly small amount of time. I gulp. I have to be strong. I can't let that grin or the rest of him sway me. I have to be strong.

When he holds out a cup, I don't take it.

"My granny called me while I was out getting coffee. She's in town and wanted to surprise me, so I thought we could have dinner tonight. With her. You could meet her."

"And…and what?" I splutter. "Give her the happy news that the fake thing isn't so fake anymore? Why would that make her happy? Why would she think I'm any different? I'm just another one in a long line of others. A…a peg or a notch or something!"

Asher's eyes darken. "That's not true."

There's such sincerity in those words that I'm totally rattled. I would have believed him if his granny hadn't been in here first and if I didn't already have a heck of a stew of doubts brewing up in my gut. And if he didn't have a long history, I didn't also have a history, and if we both knew each other for a decent amount of time before we decided to gosh darn freaking fall into bed together.

Which is actually a euphemism for having the best sex of my life.

"There's a lot on the line for me." I force my voice not to

waver because I need to be strong. And firm. And marginally angry because it's what allows me to hold on to my sanity. "I can't just jump into another relationship just like that." I have already lost three freaking years over someone who just didn't freaking care about me. I can't do that all over again. And Asher is the date and leave them kind of guy. He might be serious now but what about later on.

"Emily—"

"I think you should just leave. Please. If I'm going to have to endure dinner, then I need my space, and I need time to get ready. I have to prepare to be fake."

I can't look at Asher. I can't stand to see how I've hurt him. Maybe that's how this goes. That's the risk of not faking something. Of being real. Because being real always gets you hurt. Caring, feeling, it always sucks. That's just how it goes, and I'm no different from the next person. I should know that. I'm not special, as Asher's granny pointed out. I'm just a regular person who was plain stupid, and now I'm making my own bed. Uh, literally. I'm going to have to wash those sheets because I won't be able to stand the smell of Asher on them. Because it's a good smell. It's a very great smell, and I can't afford to think things like that. I can't afford any of this.

How did I ever get myself into this?

Oh right. With a kiss.

One kiss. Jeez, all those who say kissing leads to more, leads to destruction, damnation, and hellfire...well, they're all correct.

"Why are you...I don't understand..." Asher isn't leaving. In fact, he's still standing there. Holding the coffees that he was kind enough to get. And yup, he looks seriously confused. And seriously hurt.

I tear my eyes away, but it's too late. The soft, achy,

terrible damage has already been done. "It's just better if we go back to being fake," I rasp, and the words feel like I'm being forced to eat a barbed wire sandwich. "It's best for both of us."

"That's hardly...I...you've just decided this? Without giving me any benefit of the doubt? Without even giving me a chance? I know what my past might look like to you, and I know we don't know each other well enough for me to tell you that you can trust me, but *you can*. I haven't done anything but...but try to treat you how you deserve to be treated."

Any more of this, and I am going to melt into a puddle of tears and regret, and I can't do that. I have to be strong. I have to figure out how to get out of this somehow. How to get us both out of it with all our pieces intact.

"I just can't do it. I'm sorry."

Asher's mouth sets in a grim line. "Fine. If you want to go back to that, if you want fake, then I can give you that."

"Good. That's what I want. Fake. The plastic kind of fake. We should only have to keep it up for a few more weeks before we go our separate ways."

"Right. Well, here. You might as well have both of these. No, I didn't poison them because fake people don't feel enough emotion to even think of such a thing. Enjoy." He sets the coffees down on the dresser. "See you tonight, fake girlfriend. I'll be here to fake pick you up at fake seven to take you to eat fake food at a fake restaurant with my very real granny. I hope you're on your fake best behavior. Have a great rest of your fake morning and a great fake afternoon." Then, he pastes on a fake smile, turns, and leaves.

The door slams below me shortly after. The sound rattles through me, and my teeth knock together as I shiver.

Mr. Charming (Not)

This is exactly how I knew this would end up—in a big, nasty, out of control, flaming pile of disaster. Just like how my table went out. FML times infinity. I have no idea how to figure this out. I knew being fake would be complicated, but I had no idea. The only person I ever knew how to be, was me. I also have no idea why this fight with my fake boyfriend, who I've known for all of a little more than a week, hurts more than breaking up with Byron ever did. For the record, I was angry about what he did—humiliated and embarrassed. In the end, though, I was relieved. Relieved it was over and that I was free. I used that anger and relief to get me through, as well as axing and burning a table.

But there's none of that to carry me through this time. No anger, no relief, and no burning tables or axes. It's just me and the pain in my chest, and I'm scared it's not going to go away.

15

ASHER

The herd of journalists outside the restaurant we pull up to only adds to the list of things entitled *super shitty things that can and will get shittier in this already super shitty day that started out not so shitty but quickly descended into the vilest shittyness.*

Emily is wearing a dress from my granny's line. I know because granny told me on the phone when she told me what restaurant to meet her at. I knew it would be at seven because Granny always picks dinner for seven. I also know the dress costs three grand because granny promised she had it delivered sealed up tighter than a tight asshole—yes, she literally said that, which shocked the hell out of me. What I didn't know was that there'd be an entire horde of journalists, their cameras at the ready.

As I get out of my rental and pass the valet the keys, I have to fight my way over to Emily's door. She can't possibly be ready for this despite the fake smile she's wearing along with my granny's dress. She looks great with her long hair done up in a tight roll at the back of her head, flawless makeup, including dark eyeliner and red lipstick,

Mr. Charming (Not)

and a dress that looks stellar on an already perfect body. It's black and sparkly, cut low in the back but modest in the front, and it falls to her knees. She's wearing a pair of gold heels that make her legs look so good; I'd like to taste every inch of them.

Which makes me harder than a fucking steel beam. Because I already know how some parts of her taste. I'd like to use my tongue to memorize every detail of her, but I haven't gone that far yet.

And I probably won't be able to, based on whatever happened this morning.

I hate how Emily is hiding the fact that she's scared. And annoyed. She slips her hand into mine and smiles up at me, but it's not real. I know it's not because I've seen genuine smiles from her.

The media, though? They love it. The flashes go off with an even greater frenzy when I slip my arm around Emily's waist and guide her toward the restaurant. I press my hand against the small of her back right below where the dress is cut. She's like fire against my palm, and I have to grind my teeth. We fight through the crowd, which is mostly me sticking my arm out and carefully pushing forward. Not making contact, but demanding space as I keep the other arm wrapped protectively around Emily. It's a relief when we hit the door.

I push it open and make sure Emily gets in ahead of me. None of the journalists follow, but they'll probably be at every open window, trying to get a shot of us having dinner, though. I shudder.

I haven't had a chance to talk to her about this morning. However, I shouldn't have walked out on her like that. I don't know what she was thinking, but I got my male panties in a bit of a twist hearing her level accusations like that at me without any reason for it. It stung. It stung my pride, and it stung my erm...well, bits of me inside that I'm not so used to using. It was worse than the ego thing. A lot worse.

Emily leans in while the suited host checks the list after I give him my name. "Time to get the show on the road. The second show. The one back there was obviously the first." Her voice is thick with accusation and displeasure.

"I didn't like it either," I respond.

"Here we are. Table for three," the host says.

I drop my hand from Emily's back and motion for her to follow the host. It would obviously suit her just fine if we didn't have to touch each other for the rest of the night. Which, if there aren't any camera sharks at the windows, she might be able to get away with.

My granny stands when she sees us. She knows this is all for show, and it leaves a bad taste in my mouth when she grips Emily's hand, tugs her to herself, and places a kiss on both of her cheeks. Emily sinks down at her seat, stunned. Then, she haphazardly grabs her cloth napkin and immediately tucks it into her lap. There are glasses of water on the table, and she grabs that too, draining half of it in a single gulp before setting it down and smiling that terrible smile that doesn't even halfway reach her eyes.

I sink down in the seat across from her while granny remains at the head. Our table is in a corner, thank our lucky fortunes, or maybe Granny insisted. The rest of the place is packed, and thankfully, there are no windows around. I let out a small sigh, and I can feel my shoulders slump a little with relief.

Across the table, Emily looks like this is torture. She's so clearly unhappy.

I have no idea what happened between around three

Mr. Charming (Not)

and nine this morning when I got back from getting us coffee.

She obviously had a change of heart. Did she panic? Read something? Hear something? What happened in those twenty minutes I was away?

"You should try the steak, dear," Granny says smoothly. "It's delicious, and you can order it any way you like. And get a red to go with it. Something as great as your hair."

Emily picks up the menu and hides behind it while I shoot Granny a look. She just gives me this innocent, wide-eyed stare in response, and I slowly shake my head. She's purposely intimidating Emily. Then again, Granny probably doesn't trust her. She's never trusted a single woman I've been with as she tends to think everyone comes to the table with a shovel and bucket, ready to dig into our family gold. To be fair, she treats my mom's dates with equal suspicion.

"So." Granny folds her hands over the menu she hasn't picked up yet. "How did you two meet?"

I make a noise low in my throat that sounds like a dying coyote. "I told you, remember?" I say, but there's a warning note in my tone.

"Oh yes, right. Emily impulsively kissed you, a complete stranger, in the middle of the sidewalk."

Emily slams down her menu, and she's wearing the most poisonous smile I've ever seen. "That's right. I did," she says as she bats her eyelashes at me. "And it was the most sensual, delightful, wonderful, blissful, amazing experience of my entire life."

"Oh, sweetheart, you really need to get out more. You should come to visit me in Paris."

"You know," Emily says sweetly. "I've heard it's kind of dirty there. Like dirty money and bribery." She pegs me with a dirty look before turning and giving my granny the same.

I'm stunned. I'm not sure why Emily has taken an instant dislike to my granny, but maybe she's being punished, by extension, for being related to me.

Well, regardless, granny can definitely hold her own. "Nothing like a little bribery to get the blood flowing," she says under her breath.

Emily's eyes dart between us. "I can so tell you're both related."

At that moment, a server approaches, a middle-aged woman with gray hair tightly pulled back, a white blouse, and black pants. I know she's probably going to ask about drinks, but I'm desperate to end this meeting as soon as I can, so I blurt out something about steak and red wine. Whatever Granny had mentioned. If our server is surprised, she takes it in stride. My granny orders the same. And of course, when it gets to Emily, she demurely hands over her menu and smiles sweetly at the lady.

"I'll have the chicken. Extra garlic and onions, please. Also, a white wine. Whatever you think would go best. And the dessert menu looked fabulous." She hasn't even seen it yet. "I'll get one of everything."

After our server leaves, I let out a breath. Granny actually looks impressed.

"You know," Granny says, beaming at Emily. "I think I like you. Of all the bimbos that Asher's dated, you're the best."

"Hey!" I protest.

"Hey," Emily grunts as well.

"That was supposed to be a compliment," Granny assures us. "Now, let's talk about Paris. You seem to have some misguided notion that it's dirty. It's not dirty! It's the most fabulous city in the world. And I'll tell you why."

And just like that, I'm forgotten, completely excluded from the conversation. Granny has this crazy ability to make people both love and hate her, often at the same time. Emily is probably as confused as anything, but I watch Granny win her over right in front of me.

By the time our food comes, Emily is flushed, and she's forgotten all about being here to fake it with me. Instead, she's hanging on Granny's every word. Her eyes are bright, and she looks excited as the server slides a huge plate of chicken in front of her.

"Maybe I would like to go," she confesses. "You make it sound amazing."

"Oh, it is," Granny assures her. "You could come as my special guest whenever you like. I have a private jet at my disposal, so it's no problem to pick you up."

"Could I bring someone?"

Granny gives me a sidelong glance.

"I mean my parents. They'd adore it. Or maybe a friend? I have a couple who would die to go."

"Of course. You just let me know. By the way, the chicken looks divine. Want to switch?"

Emily, who was so against the suggestion of steak and ordered chicken probably just to spite my granny, neatly slides her plate over, picking Granny's up as she goes along. She switches the wines out too.

What the actual heck? My granny is freaking made of rainbows, unicorn farts, flying monkeys, avocados with hearts instead of pits, and happy sloths. She's trendy, beautiful, dignified, and she has this magic power I lack.

Powers that can get Emily to like her.

I thought I had that power. For once in my life, I finally

just felt free to be me. To just spend a night with a woman I wanted to spend a night with and have that desire reciprocated with no demands whatsoever. There should have been something there—demands, I mean, seeing as what we'd already established, but there wasn't, and I have no clue how to get that Emily back. The Emily from last night. The Emily who laughs at fart stories and gets teary-eyed about her family and opera. The Emily who covered me up when I fell asleep on her couch. The funny, witty, happy Emily who didn't mysteriously very much dislike me.

She knew all that stuff about me before, yet it didn't change what she wanted last night. That's all I can reason as I cut and chew the most delicious steak I've had in a long time. I can tell it's good even though my mood is ruining it. I fall into a rhythm. Cut, chew. Cut, chew. Cut, chew. All while Emily and Granny talk and laugh like I'm not even here.

When we're done eating, Emily pushes her plate away, and Granny winks at her. "The desserts are on me."

"Oh, believe me, I know," Emily says, and they both laugh like it's hilarious that Emily ordered an entire menu just for spite.

"Share it with your family and friends. There's probably going to be a lot of boxes for you to take out, so have them deliver it! It will be easier for you."

What. On. Fucking. Planet. Fucking. Earth. Is. Happening?

"Be a dear, Asher, and pick up the tab." Granny grips my hand and squeezes. "I'm going to slip out the back and beat all those farging photographers at their own game. I've been walking around in disguise all day, but it wouldn't have done to show up to dinner wearing a sack and a wig, walking all hunched over."

Mr. Charming (Not)

"Please tell me that's not how you went out earlier."

"I did! That's why it's so great to have pink hair. Everyone looks for it. I slap a head of gray curls on and bam! I'm no longer Julie Louise Paris. I'm just some other old lady. And I came prepared." She cackles at the next bit. "I bought some fast fashion and put it on!"

"You didn't!" Emily gasps. "That's hardly ethical."

"Well, don't worry. I got it from a used site. Someone was selling quite a bit of their wardrobe for almost nothing. It was quite the score. Is it so bad if it's second hand?"

Emily groans. "I'm not sure. If you saved it from a landfill, then maybe it's not so bad."

"I most certainly did then." Granny nods, first at me, then at Emily. "Enjoy your night, dear. I'm flying back to Paris tomorrow." Next, she turns and faces Emily. "And you. Enjoy your desserts. You're quite an unexpected delight. Lots of pluck. I like that." She stands, spryer than a twenty-year-old. "Here." She places something in Emily's hand. "This is for you." Then, she practically sprints off toward the back of the restaurant before either of us can say anything.

Emily glances at whatever it is Granny just handed her, and I swear she goes pale as she quickly tucks it into her purse. I have no idea what just happened, though that's pretty much been my mantra during the entire dinner.

"What was—" I start, but I'm interrupted as our server shows up to clear away the plates.

"How would you like those desserts? I'm assuming you'd like them packaged up?"

Emily looks a little bit guilty now. "Uh, oh. I...could I get them delivered?"

The poor server looks as confused as a camel in the Arctic. They don't have camels up there, do they? But she recovers fast. "Oh. Certainly. You can just give me your information, and I'll have it taken care of."

"Thanks." Emily rattles off her address, and the lady writes it down.

I whip out a handful of cash and pass it over. There's enough of a tip there to make up for our unconventional dinner. She walks off, a renewed and pleasant expression on her face.

"What did she give you?" I ask, uninterrupted this time.

It's not my imagination. Emily truly does look pale. "You know," she whispers. "I think I'm going to do like your granny did and sneak out the back way and get into one of those taxis waiting out front. I will ask the the staff to request that one be brought out back. All those photographers were pretty intense, and if they're still out there, I'd rather not face them. You should probably wait five minutes and do the same. Beat them at their own game."

"You're assuming they're not covering the back way."

"Oh. Shit." Emily clutches her purse tight. The urge to try and wrestle it away from her and look at what Granny passed over is so strong that I have to fight it down. Because it would certainly make me the biggest asshole of the century. "Well, I guess I'll take my chances."

"Emily..."

"What?" She pauses, half out of her chair.

She looks like an ethereal goddess in my granny's dress. Although she'd look just as gorgeous in sweats and a baggy, stained t-shirt, I'm sure. I want to say something, the right thing, the thing that would fix things, but it just won't come. I don't know if it even exists.

"Can we talk?" I let that pathetic statement hang in the air.

"I..." Emily hesitates. She's still levitating out of her

Mr. Charming (Not)

chair. "Tomorrow. But...but not about this. About us. It's safer this way. To not get involved like we were. For both of us."

"Safer?"

"They're probably going to deliver the desserts to my house soon, so I should probably be there," Emily mutters as she flies out of her chair and scuttles off toward the back. I want to follow her, and I want to beg her to tell me what happened, why she's suddenly running from me, metaphorically and literally.

Our server magically appears back at the table. She has something in her hand, which I realize is the receipt for the dinner. I don't even glance at it. I do realize the lady—god, I should have gotten her name, I'm sure she said it at some point, probably before the meal—is giving me some sort of sympathetic look, so maybe I look as shitty as I feel. I know that in my suit, I look just fine, but my face or eyes or something is giving away my inner turmoil. In addition to the shit sandwich of a day, there was something *distinctly* not right about dinner.

That was the strangest dinner I've ever had to sit through. And now I'm here. Alone. As both my own grandmother and Emily have scrambled off.

"You look like you could use a dessert yourself."

I don't eat dessert, but instead of stating that, I just nod. "Whatever you think is the best. I'll have one of those."

"Definitely the chocolate cake. It's my favorite. Always cheers me up when I'm in a bad mood. Not that it's stress eating. It's good at any time. But it's the best when, you know, you need to eat a few feelings."

Well prickly pears, am I that obvious? "Thanks. That's great."

After, when I'm truly alone, I sit there and fold the

receipt into tiny little squares. I don't even like chocolate. Cherry cheesecake would have been a much better choice, but that's alright. If it's good for eating the feelings, then I'll eat it.

Feelings.

I don't exactly know what to do with those.

I can't say I've ever really had to think about it very hard before. Or fight. I haven't fought for anyone. Ever. All I had in the past were interludes with women who were equally not looking for something serious or women whose only interests were on my bank account. Generally speaking, I've never even wanted more in life.

It's hard for me to remember why I did not try harder. Why everything was so superfluous. In fact, it's hard for me to remember anything at all. Because when I try, I just picture Emily.

I guess I need that chocolate cake even more than I already thought.

16

EMILY

I know where I went wrong. It was that first minute where I thought I could hold out against Asher. Because if I had just caved and said I was sorry for kissing him, then kissed my ass goodbye, quit my job, sold my house, and I don't know, lived as a hermit or something in the middle of nowhere or maybe took up residence in my parents' nasty old basement right beside the mouse colonies and infestation of fist-waving spiders, I never would have had to risk getting attached.

Even after a week and several granny warnings, which I'm not entirely sure actually apply after last night's dinner, there's a kernel of something there which I'm pretty sure is —*holy craptacular crap*—*the fact that I think I like Asher despite everything, or maybe because of everything, for real.*

And now there's a heck of a lot of dust in my eyes.

I need to call someone—a friend, my parents, or my brothers. I need to talk, and I need to figure this out. The thing Asher's granny forced into my hand last night? It was a cheque. Also, there is a heck of a lot of desserts clogging up my fridge that need to be eaten, and it's not like I can load them up and donate them down the street to the people sitting there the way I did with Byron's laptop and my engagement ring.

Yeah, I really gave the laptop away as well. A person who takes an ax to a table and sets it on fire doesn't kid about that kind of stuff.

I'm busy with my phone—scrolling through contacts and calculating the odds of finding someone at home on a Sunday afternoon—when my doorbell rings.

I actually cringe. Lately, the doorbell hasn't been a very good thing, but I relax, knowing it's not ninja granny out there because she would just walk right in. And if the door were locked, she'd jerry-rig it and get it open in no time. There doesn't seem to be anything Julie Louise Paris can't do, including making me like her.

I think she even kind of felt bad about what she said about Asher. She probably had her spies report that we spent the night together, freaked out, and flew all the way from Paris. However, that would have taken a considerable amount of time, which possibly means she never left St. Louis after the first time she paid me a visit. And as such, it could mean that maybe she's the spy.

The idea of a tiny, pink-haired old lady dressed all in black and using a set of binoculars to look through my window makes me want to laugh, but it also unnerves me. I wouldn't put anything past her since she's astoundingly spry for her age. She could still kick some serious ass.

When I think about my own grandmothers compared with Asher's, it makes me smile. One of them is thoroughly attached to her fuzzy pink slippers, and she wears band t-shirts all day long, while the other's perm has always given her an extra six or so odd inches of height because she backcombs her backcomb on top of the curly perm.

Mr. Charming (Not)

There's no messing with Grandma Paige's perms. Don't get between her and her hairdressing appointments, or watch out! Anyway, neither of them is very spry, and neither would resort to blackmail. Also, neither of them would try to charm me into going to Paris on their private jet because neither of them has a private jet. But even if they did...

Anyway, half of me wonders if Asher's granny tried to win me over because she thought it would be fun to toy with me as she believes in keeping her enemies close or because she was genuinely sorry about showing up at my house like a granny ghost of grannies past and scaring the living peanut butter and jelly out of me.

I can't think about this anymore because I have to get the door. Plus, if I do any more thinking, I'm scared the top of my head will tear off and go rocketing into the ceiling. Or that I'll just explode like my fridge jammed full of desserts.

Maybe it's my mom. It would be perfect if it were my mom, surprising me. We could eat cake, pie, or cheesecake and talk about all this fake stuff morphing into something I don't understand.

But no.

When I open the door, it's Asher. Casual Asher, dressed in jeans and a t-shirt. The only difference is he's not grinning at me like he usually is when I find him out here. Instead, he jams the toe of his black boot into the door, and I back up, ready to throw down.

"Are you really sticking your toe into my door so I can't close it on you?"

"Yup. I was afraid you'd do that."

"I could break your toe, you know."

"Unlikely. These are steel-toed boots."

I eye them up and scoff, "No, they're not."

"They are," he insists.

"They're not. Why would you have steel-toed boots?"

"Touché. I'm a liar, and I'm lying about that. I've lied a lot in my life, about all manner of things. I've lied to my granny, to my mom, to friends, and certainly to any and all forms of media. I've lied about my life so many times that I've lost track. I've lied to employers and employees, to professors, my teachers before that, to other instructors, to…to just about everyone at some time or other. You're the only person I haven't lied to. Not that I'm a chronic liar. Because I'm not. I'm just being brutally honest here. And half of those were white lies. The kind of thing where someone asks if their dress looks great on them, and you know it doesn't, but you lie because you don't want to be a total jackass and tell them so. But I'm not a bad person. I know I've been made out to be a player, and I haven't taken many relationships seriously…for a lot of reasons, half of which you already know. The other half, I can only say I was young and not ready and also fairly stupid, as young men usually are. The best thing that has happened to me, easily, in the past, let's say a solid five years, is that kiss you gave me on the sidewalk. Also for many reasons, which I'm sure you don't know. This wasn't supposed to become legit. I don't even really know what that means if we're being honest here, which I am. I just know the time I've spent with you has been really, really good. Awesome, actually. I get why you panicked and freaked out. I get it because I took a good look at myself and my past and all the reasons you have not to trust me. I never wanted to hurt you. You are like this pearl. A rare pearl. A big and huge one. The most valuable…never mind. That's bad. I read it somewhere, comparing women to pearls, but that's not a good thing. You're not a pearl, and you're not cold or stony or silent. You're real. You're just...you're you, and you have no idea how much I appreciate that."

Asher finally stops and takes a breath. He takes several, actually. That was probably the longest speech I've ever heard anyone make, and it makes me feel mushy. Both bad and good mushy. The good mushy that gets you all excited because it's a mushy day in spring after a long and treacherous winter, and you finally have hope of it getting nice out again after just nonsense cold for so long. But also the bad mushy. Like really craving a juicy pear and biting into it only to find out it's all mealy, mushy, and nasty. So. Disappointing.

I don't know what to say, but I do have a lot of desserts in my fridge, so I hear myself say, "Do you want to come in for cake? Or pie?"

Asher nods slowly. "I don't normally eat dessert, but I think I can make an exception. Again."

"What are you talking about?" I find myself caving, and I know my rationale is cracking. My firmness is also cracking, cracking around all the hard edges because I don't really have hard edges at all. And now I'm cracking a smile.

"I had dessert last night after you both left. Alone."

"You didn't!"

"I did. Our server upsold me like a boss. Although, maybe that one was on the house because I think I'd already paid and tipped well. And I must have looked pretty sorry because she said I needed to eat my feelings."

I slap a hand over my mouth. "Oh my god."

"I needed to hear it."

"No, you didn't." Asher steps in, shut the door behind him, and I deflate. It's embarrassing how badly I want to wrap my arms around his neck and press myself against him. "I'm sorry. That dinner was...I don't even know what it was. I was not in a good mood, and then I...I wasn't expecting to like your grandma, but I discovered I did, and I was still all worked up about things. I was mad at you." It sounds so silly saying it now, and it's hard for me to remember why I was mad in the first place.

Oh right. Because his granny reminded me that I was probably just another bang and bung for him. I don't know what bung is, but it sounds like one and done.

"I noticed there was a weird tension at dinner. You had no reason not to like my granny, except that she was an extension of me."

That's not it at all. Thinking about Asher's granny makes my heart skitter with dread. I might grudgingly like the woman, but I'm still basically a double agent, and I know Asher would be so hurt if he found out about the cheque in my purse. Which I'm going to rip up. I just couldn't make myself do it yesterday, so it's still in there—a twenty thousand dollar taunt—burning through my poor purse and waiting for the ax and fire, except in this case, it'll just get my hands and the garbage can.

"I'm sorry I freaked out." This, at least, I can deal with right now. "I was thinking about your past. I should have sat down and told you I was freaking out and explained everything. I don't know. You were right. You didn't deserve it, I wasn't being fair, and you always have been overly nice to me. Everyone has things they've done that they wish they hadn't done."

"Really?" He seems surprised, and I'm not sure if it's the lead-up to my admission or if he didn't expect I could be persuaded to think otherwise.

I bob my head. "Yeah. For example, I myself dated a guy for three years, someone I wasn't even in love with, and I got engaged to him. My friends were relieved when we

Mr. Charming (Not)

broke up, and I think my parents were too. I haven't even talked to them about it yet. Not *really* anyway because I don't know what to say. Is being with someone like that because you're too afraid of rejection or being alone any better than dating more people because you're young and don't really know what you want?"

It's not an open-ended question, so Asher just studies me. His eyes look a thousand shades darker blue than they ever have. After a few moments, he says, "We can only do what we're taught, I guess. And teach what we know. I don't want to use that as an excuse, but I'm ashamed to admit I have no idea what love actually looks like. Not that kind of love, at least. My granny has loved my mom and me no matter what, and there were some definitive *what* moments in there, but that's not the kind of love I mean, even if it is invaluable. I know how to love my family and how to stick together and fight it out, but I don't know anything more than that."

What he says makes me pause. I always had the benefit of seeing that my parents were in love. I knew they were, even if they didn't kiss, hug, and do the sappy stuff in front of us very often. More importantly, they provided a stable home, taught us right from wrong, looked after us, and truly cared about us.

Asher leans against the wall. "Has anything we've done felt forced to you? Awkward? Fake?"

"No," I admit on instinct, caught off guard by the change of subject, but I know I'm right. "Not even that first kiss." *Damn it*. I should have kept that bit to myself.

"Not even that first kiss," he echoes in agreement.

Holy dingleberries, I think we just made up. Or maybe that's some kind of cue because Asher steps forward, and I find myself closing the distance, reaching for him, craving his arms, his closeness, his presence, and the feel of his body pressed up and wrapped around mine. I crave his scent, which by now, I know by heart. Which then gets my heart pumping and my blood flowing. And also my lady berries berrying if you know what I mean. Maybe temptation, loss of control, and bad decisions aren't so bad after all.

Or maybe that's just my brain short-circuiting out because my hands land on Asher's chest, and I lift my chin as he claims my mouth. And no, this doesn't feel anything less than one hundred million, billion, trillion, gazillion percent the greatest, smartest, most genuine idea in the world.

17

ASHER

I sweep Emily into my arms like the gallant knight rescuing his damsel in distress. Also, it's just amazing to have Emily in my arms, especially with her hands locked around my neck and her lips locked with mine.

"Shower," she rasps. "Upstairs."

Alright, we might also have an aversion to beds it seems.

I head up the stairs while Emily attacks my mouth. Her tongue demands war, and my tongue gives in easily. My balls have crept up with every single step until they feel lodged in my throat, whereas my dick is back to being weapon-worthy.

I set Emily down just inside her bathroom. It's fairly large, with an older-style glass shower that's separate from the tub. Just the sight of it makes my dick ache, and I want to do dirty, raw, and sensual things to her in there.

Emily's hands immediately duck under my t-shirt, and I help her slip it off. I go for her blouse next, and while she battles with her leggings, I slide my jeans down. She stops her undressing at the good part, leaving her bra and panties on for me. They're not a matching set, just a plain white bra and black panties, but they're hot as sin anyway.

Taking me a little off guard, she leans forward, sets her hands on my chest, and circles my nipple with her tongue. I didn't realize my nipples had a lot of sensation, but when Emily licks them, they certainly do. I feel the stirring sensations all the way to my balls, and she falls to her knees before I've even fully registered the pleasure radiating out from my nipple. Then, she tugs my boxers down, freeing my cock, and it springs up, nearly smacking her in the face. Thank god the bastard misses.

Emily giggles. Also, thank god she thinks it's amusing. Her hand wraps around my shaft, and I lose the smile fast. I close my eyes when she moves her sweet, tight hand from the tip of my dick to my balls. Her other palm remains flat on my stomach, and she leans forward, taking me so far into her mouth that she coughs. She slowly withdraws as I tangle my fingers in her hair and let out the world's deepest groan.

"You don't have to—"

"Shh," she commands, and her warm breath makes me shiver. "Stop talking."

I can do that. I can seriously do that. So I let her take the lead as she continues licking and suckling me, pumping me with her hand, swirling her tongue over my swollen tip, and taking me so far back into her throat that I see stars. She keeps going until I can barely contain it. Until I seriously doubt I can contain it. As in, I'm in total danger here. Of not containing things.

"Shower," I command, but it's more like a thready exhale.

Emily raises her head. She looks at me, her pupils fully

blown, and she must understand because she reluctantly gets up. "Okay."

She switches the taps on while I get a condom out of my jeans pocket. I quickly tear it open and slide it on. Then, I turn around, expecting Emily to be waiting patiently for me, but she's already in the shower. Already soaking wet with water sluicing over her white bra, dampening it until her dark nipples are on full display. The water hugs her curves as it flows over her body, and I long to lap up each and every single drop.

While she's watching me, Emily reaches around and unhooks her bra, and as her bra falls away, revealing two perfect breasts, she never breaks eye contact. She slowly peels her panties away next, stepping out of them one leg at a time before tossing them on the floor with a wet plop.

She beckons me forward with a finger, and holy shit, where did the shy Emily from the beginning of last night go? I do realize she's still there, in the blush that creeps up from her collarbones and spreads across her neck, and in the way her lips part and eyelashes flutter.

I step into the shower, straight into the spray. The warm water feels like heaven, but it's nothing compared to how intoxicatingly beautiful Emily is, how smooth her skin feels, and how silky and warm and wet she is between her legs.

I run my fingers over her, feeling how slick and ready she is. She wraps her arms around my neck, and I lift her on instinct to back her up against the glass wall. Her back makes a shower angel against the steamy glass as her mouth attacks mine, and my dick throbs painfully against her stomach because no, I didn't line it up properly.

Impatiently, I quickly adjust myself with one hand while I hold on to her with the other. She wriggles against me, moaning out loud when I push up against her entrance.

"God, you're so thick," she whimpers.

Her words make my dick jerk so hard that I just about don't make it another second. My balls have turned the purplest shade of purple that ever existed. With a groan, I break the kiss and look right into her eyes. Her pupils are still massive, her eyes dark and liquid, filled with trust, hope, vulnerability, and both confidence and uncertainty. Emily is a mystery I'll never unravel. I'm certain of it. It makes me want to try, though. It makes me want to spend a lifetime trying.

"Are you going to stick it in?" Emily asks me while I'm looking her right in the eyes.

I can't keep a rather undignified sounding snort of laughter in. "Yes," I rasp between clenched teeth because I'm trying not to laugh again. "If you want me to."

"I think that would be quite nice as I've been thinking about it for a considerable amount of time."

"I thought you were mad at me."

"Well, I was." She frowns. "But being mad didn't stop me from thinking about it, though. Anger sex or whatever they call it. I'm not angry now, though, so I think you've lost the opportunity for that. But just regular sex is still nice."

"Yes," I grind out. "Yes, it is."

I push into her slowly, letting her get used to my length. We might have done this before but she's physically tight and much smaller than me, and I don't want to hurt her with My Dragon And Mythical Monster Vanquisher. What? It seems like a cool name for my dick if I was to really use it as a weapon.

I now know what real bliss feels like. *Real*, because this is. Real. All of it. There's even a feeling attached to it. A deep sensation that sits heavily in my chest and the pit of my gut, and while it's unfamiliar, it's not entirely uncomfortable. There is absolutely no urge to run from it, from this, or from her.

I gently thrust while Emily swivels her hips away from the glass shower wall and into me. I drop my head and worship her breasts, suckling on her nipples while I continue to thrust slowly. I want to drag this out because sex in the shower isn't anything that should be rushed, but with Emily already clenching around me, her head thrown back and muscles tense and straining, I know it's not going to last more than a few more seconds.

I'm exactly right because when Emily tenses completely, then throws her head forward and sinks her teeth lightly into my shoulder while shuddering, chanting my name, and coming apart around me, I can't hold back. I think I used to have some kind of stamina, but I guess that's part of yesteryear long gone, which is maybe okay. Because when I bury myself in Emily and come with her name on my tongue, I have zero regrets.

We pant together, waiting for the shivering and spasms and heavy breathing to pass in the warm shower.

"How many of those did you bring?" Emily asks.

I finally realize what she's really asking, so I reply, "Don't worry. I have enough to last us well into the morning."

"Does that mean you're going to spend it here? Again?"

"If you'll allow me."

"It's still early. Like, really early. It's daylight out there. I'm not protesting what we're doing as long as we take food breaks. And water breaks. Because it's important to stay hydrated. I just want to make sure you really did come prepared."

"I'm fairly exhausted from the other night as we didn't sleep much." I can't hold a straight face. I have to grin. "You've worn me out, so we might spend most of those hours actually sleeping."

She slowly shakes her head at me, grinning. "We'll see. But if one of us has to run to the store, we should also do it now."

"I'm good."

"I thought you thought I was mad at you. Were you anticipating seducing me into forgiving you?"

"Never. I just thought you'd accept my sincere words and want to immediately leap into the shower and then take things next door."

"Next door?"

"To your bedroom. Or if you'd like me to prepare you a snack, naked, I can do that, just for you. There are still a ton of desserts around here, so we could incorporate them in. I wouldn't mind licking whipped cream off you."

Emily shudders against me, shivering in the good kind of way that awakens every single nerve ending I have. "I could also stand that," she whispers. "But first, if you'd be so kind as to soap me up and give me a nice back massage while we still have hot water, I'd be eternally grateful."

At that, my dick roars to life. Emily feels it and kisses me, a wicked smile on her lips.

18

ASHER

I know I should be sleeping and not playing Mr. Snoopy Snoopsalot, but when I wake up in the middle of the night, the first thing I think of is that I never asked Emily what my granny gave her. I wanted to, but I totally forgot because of...well...other things.

Emily is sleeping soundly right beside me. I should just stay here, wrap myself around her, and hold her. I should forget about whatever it was Granny pressed into her hand.

But I can't.

Lying here thinking about it feels a little bit like sitting in that theatre with a gas explosion building in my belly. No, slow leaks weren't an option, and I can't just expel the idea and be done with it.

When I slide out of bed and find my boxers, I do feel like a bastard.

And when I slip downstairs, all silent and lethal like, I feel more like a cloud of stench spreading through the house. What I'm about to do, stinks alright.

I stop in the kitchen to think. The brand new table is still lying neatly where I stacked it after it collapsed. I really should find someone—a professional carpenter or something—and pay them to put it together. The ax is nowhere in sight, so it must have been relegated to a closet somewhere. The garage? Is there a basement? A crawlspace?

Through the darkness outside, I can make out the shape of the brand new fence. The crew I hired worked wonders back there.

If I was something tiny and folded up, where would I hide? Or maybe just something tiny. Something flat? Round? Paper? Metal?

Granny could have given Emily anything. A piece of jewelry to wear because it would look like I had given it to her instead? Because maybe Granny thought I was too dense to think of that. It could have been a folded-up piece of paper with Granny's phone number on it, a business card, a freaking tissue. Anything.

Why am I even down here?

I grab a glass of water and start back upstairs, but then I see it. On the sideboard hutch thing beyond where the table is piled.

Emily's purse.

I know from much experience that a woman's purse is off-limits. Like, put your foot in a loaded spring trap kind of off-limits, don't touch a rattlesnake kind of off-limits. It's common sense. I've never in my life snooped through anything that didn't belong to me, let alone a purse.

But I still find myself setting my glass of water on the counter and tiptoeing across the vinyl flooring over to the hutch. The purse is plain, a square of dark brown soft leather with a long handle. I run my fingers over the smooth surface and sigh.

Mr. Charming (Not)

This is low. Like crust of the earth low, magma low, and whatever is at the center below that low.

But still, I pop the snap that keeps it closed from the inside and hold it up to the light. There isn't much in there. It's remarkably clean. Just a wallet, a pair of sunglasses, car keys, and a little pocket with a spare pack of tissues.

The wallet. It sucks me in like a freaking black vortex of evilness. The wallet is soft leather like the purse, though it doesn't exactly match as it's a shade lighter. I know they weren't purchased together, which might be freaky, but then again, I have a grandmother in fashion.

My hands visibly shake, and my buttocks clench up as I pop open her wallet, which is held together by a snap too. There's Emily's driver's license, credit cards, other IDs, some other cards, blah, blah, blah. Just the regular wallet stuff. The folded pockets in the wallet contain a twenty-dollar bill, two old receipts, a coupon for organic milk, and a smoothed-out, crumpled-up rectangle. It's facing the wrong way, but I can't stop myself now. I'm already the nastiest of the nasty just by looking in here, so I take a deep breath, grip the rectangle, and pull it out before turning it around.

As soon as I see the name, I drop it. The wallet too. The purse follows, and everything goes clattering to the floor. In the silent house, it's as loud as a cannon blasting through the room.

I pause, hold my breath, and don't budge a single muscle.

When I hear footsteps from upstairs, soft steps that barely make a sound, I don't stop and gather up the evidence. I don't frantically put it all back and grab my glass of water to pretend I was doing nothing on top of nothing down here.

Emily appears, with her hair tangled around her face, sleep in her eyes, and sheet creases on her cheeks. She's thrown a robe on—a massive purple thing with a tail and a face on the other side that dwarfs her.

She freezes when she sees me, and her hand flies to her throat like she just choked on a fishbone that appeared out of nowhere. Her breath catches with a loud mmmmmm-phrfp, and my eyes fly from her purse and wallet on the floor back up to her face. She pales, then she steps forward, grabs my glass of water, and drains it.

"What the heck is that?" I point down to the floor vaguely, but she knows. She knows what I found.

"I...Asher...I didn't cash it. I was going to tear it up. Truly."

"I don't really care what you were going to do with it. I want to know why you have it. Why did my granny give you a cheque for twenty thousand dollars?" I'm pretty sure it wasn't done out of the goodness of her heart. My granny might be spontaneous, but she didn't sit at the table right in front of me and write out a cheque. Which means she brought it to the dinner and had it ready. Why?

"It's not...she..."

"Are you playing both sides now, Emily?" It's the first thing that comes to mind, and it's truly terrible, like someone throwing darts at a dartboard but missing and hitting my nuts instead. Basically, it's quite incapacitating.

Her mouth drops open, and the stain of scarlet on her cheeks is immediate. Her eyes dart from mine to the purse, then back up. I've never seen her look guilty before, but she looks guilty now. "She wanted me to fake date you," she blurts. "The same thing you wanted. She contacted me first. She wanted me to be prepared for you to show up and

Mr. Charming (Not)

ask me. I also didn't want to lose my job. I've worked really, really hard for it."

My stomach feels like I just had really sharp, jagged-edged rocks for breakfast, lunch, and dinner the past month. "And the twenty grand was just a bonus?"

"I was going to tear it up. It wasn't about that. I...everything just turned into such craziness. One second I kissed you, and the next, your granny showed up at my door, and she was...I guess pretty convincing the way she is, and she told me not to tell you. She wanted you to get settled, to have something steady for a while, and to have someone behind you. Someone who was boring and normal and not..."

"And she thought it would be best for me to have someone in my corner, someone who was just pretending to be there? Because she was getting paid and wanted to keep her job?"

"No! I don't know what she thought. It was weird. Both times she's showed up here, it was weird." She slaps a hand over her mouth.

Both times. Granny was in town yesterday. "She came here? When I was out getting coffee?"

"Y...yes."

"And tried to warn you off because she thought things were getting too real?"

"B...basically." Emily's eyes are huge, and I ignore the sheen of moisture in them. Maybe she does feel bad. Perhaps she isn't faking that. Maybe what she felt was genuine attraction, but I'm beyond trying to pick out bits and pieces to analyze whether they were real or not. "I'm not going to try to tell you it was right. It was definitely not right. Your granny kind of scared me, but I think she truly was trying to look out for you and give you a new start somewhere else with a fresh chance to experience something different. She knew you'd be pissed if you found out. I knew too, and I should have told you that she contacted me. Twice. I should have...I just...I didn't. I felt like I'd be betraying her."

"Do you have any idea how crazy all of this is? You and her? She's done some pretty wild things before, but nothing even close to this."

"Asher! It...I really...we...it wasn't contrived. The dates were one thing, but this...this was real. For me."

"I know," I sigh. "I know it was." I think I can still tell the difference between real affection and something forced, and I don't think Emily is capable of pretending. She's not a good actress. Everything she feels is always right on her face, which is why I can't look there at the moment. "But it doesn't really matter. Yesterday, you said you couldn't trust me because of my past, but I can't trust you either. Our chemistry might be good, but that's all it is. People can fit together really well physically and still be a disaster in every other way, which won't work. I've seen that. Especially with my mom. So I know it's true."

"Please wait. Please, just sit down and talk. I can make tea, and we can figure it—"

"We can't. It's only been a week, and look at the disaster right now. It would probably only get worse and worse until it explodes and hurts other people too. Maybe feeling nothing is best because everything else is just complicated and won't work."

"No! That's exactly what your granny didn't want you to think."

"Then she went about it the wrong way. Cash the cheque if you want, and you'll still keep your job. She had no right to threaten to fire you, and I would never do

Mr. Charming (Not)

that. Anyway, I hope we can be good coworkers in the future."

"Asher—"

"I'd really like to get my clothes. If that's okay."

"No! It's not okay!" Emily moves to stand in my path.

Suddenly, I realize she's wearing a purple cat robe. There are ears and a face on the hood, which explains the long tail at the back. She looks so freaking adorable standing there blocking my way that I do feel myself caving. I wouldn't mind talking it out, staying, and taking her back up to bed, which is entirely the wrong response for someone whose granny and girlfriend—one who was fake, then not so fake, then kind of conspiring, then off, then on again, then not so fake, or maybe fake after all—were conspiring against him since the start.

Even if it was supposed to end up well. Even if my granny had good intentions. My head feels like it's going to explode like an angry shaken soda at the moment, and I'm sure Emily wasn't explaining things well because she's stressed. I think my granny just wanted me to be happy, and this really wasn't Emily's fault, and maybe...*wow, what a mess.*

"It's not okay," Emily repeats. "I don't want you to leave like this. Not upset and not in the middle of the night. You're tired. Don't drive like that."

Her concern is real, and it shames me. I've left more times in the middle of the night than I can count. Most of the time, it's because I wasn't expected to stay until morning, but Emily doesn't even go there. She doesn't even think it because she's a good person.

"We should call your grandma and get her to come over and explain everything. We should sit down and talk, so please, stay until the morning. We can call her then.

Even if we don't end up...*together*," she forces that word out, "at least we won't be angry with each other. Or with your grandma. I know how much she means to you. She really was just trying to protect you—both times when she came here."

"By poisoning the well and hiring a girlfriend behind my back?" I hold up a hand and stop myself. "Okay, sorry. You're right. You're right, and I appreciate your offer." I realize how much bravery it took her to extend it, and I truly do appreciate it. That Emily can own up to what she did, doesn't make excuses, and still wants to make things right, not just for her but for my granny and me.

"I have a guest room made up," she goes on, her voice soft. I can tell she's trying to keep the sadness out of it. "So you may sleep there until it's a decent hour to call her. I don't doubt she's still here even if she said she was leaving."

"I think you're right. Maybe she has been keeping tabs on me the whole time because it sounds like something she'd do."

"So you won't leave?"

"I'll take the guest room," I say, giving in.

Emily lets out a massive sigh of relief, and her fuzzy shoulders heave and cave. Her face is a mix of relief, sadness, despair, loss, pain, hurt, remorse, and maybe even a little bit of hope. I can't imagine what mine gives away, so I glance down at her purse and wallet.

I pick it up and put it neatly back on the shelf as a sort of apology. I wonder if she would have told me, given time. Most probably. Because I know Emily is a good person. I just know it. She cares, and she's the kind of person who makes sure everyone is okay before she is. She can admit her faults, she says things no one else would say, and she's this incredible package. I know all those things with

Mr. Charming (Not)

certainty, and I don't need more time to figure it out. So yes, she probably would have told me after she ripped up the cheque. She would have waited for the right moment when I wouldn't get mad at my granny, and she would have explained everything, making me understand.

So maybe there's some hope on my face too.

This is the first time I haven't left because it's easier to just leave. This is the first time I've wanted to stay, even if it's messy and uncomfortable. And that says something.

I let Emily go on ahead so it won't be extremely awkward upstairs. I figure the guest room is up there, too, since the hallway had other doors. I climb the steps, and with each one, I feel more and more exhausted. It's obviously not just the physical lack of sleep weighing me down.

I push open doors until I find a room with a bed. There are only three besides Emily's, and I get it right on the first try, by process of elimination—I knew the door beside Emily's bedroom is the bathroom—and some luck.

There's an extra blanket at the foot of the double bed with the white metal headboard and footboard. It could have been there before, but I don't think so. No, I know for sure Emily just put it there.

Because, of course, she'd push down her own pain and sadness and think about something like that.

About me.

19

EMILY

I didn't think I'd be able to sleep after the late-night fiasco in my kitchen.

But yes, I'm awake now.

Because five minutes ago, a knock at my bedroom door woke me up. It was immediately followed by Asher's deep voice informing me that his granny would be at my house in about five minutes, which gives me about four minutes to try and pull myself together, cover up the massive purple bags under my eyes, get rid of the red rim accompanying the said purple bags, and put on something decent.

By decent, I mean fair trade clothing that Asher's granny is going to scorn, but then again, I'm not exactly worried about her opinion at the moment.

I should have told Asher. Indeed, I would have if I weren't so intimidated by his granny. I think that given a few more weeks, I would have worked up the nerve. I would never have cashed that cheque. Not after Asher was so generous. I probably would have contacted his granny first to tell her that I was going to tell him and to announce I wasn't afraid of her and her threats to fire me. Well, I

Mr. Charming (Not)

honestly still would have been, but I would have stated I wasn't.

Finding that cheque was the worst thing Asher could have done. I'm not sure why his granny gave it to me at dinner when he could obviously see and have his curiosity piqued. It never slipped his mind, and he went looking to see what it was. If only I had shredded it and thrown it out like I wanted to. Why did I wait?

Anyway, the damage is done now. Asher will probably never trust me again. I couldn't string two sentences together last night to save my soul and give him a decent explanation. His hurt was obvious, as was his anger at finding out that I was playing both sides, which is what he termed it. And yet, he still stayed the night. He's still here.

I don't know how long it's going to last, so as I slide on a pair of leggings and a tunic from last year's sports line—my favorite one though, so I own every single piece from it because it's comfortable—I vow to get my shit together. Not just my shit, but the parts that aren't shit too—all the 'unshitty' shit.

I pull my hair into a high bun on top of my head, swatch on a bunch of foundation, and stumble downstairs. Even though the makeup won't help my bloodshot, red-rimmed eyes, because yes, I kind of did cry myself back to sleep, it might do wonders for the bags, tired lines, and regret oozing from every pore.

Asher has a pot of coffee going. He is truly a walking, living, breathing miracle. I also can't believe he knows how to operate a coffee maker because no one I've ever lived with before—minus my parents, but they don't count—has ever been able to do that.

He's sitting on the blue couch in the living room,

sipping on a cup, and there's one waiting for me on the coffee table—black, which is just how I like it.

"How do you know how I take my coffee?" I recall the ones he left at my house yesterday morning, which feels like approximately six thousand stone ages ago. Is that even a term? One of them had cream while the other was black.

"At work. You have a mug of black coffee sitting on your desk. Half drunk and always halfway there. Then you pour it out and get a refresher. Like the bottom half just isn't as good as the top.

"It really isn't. And warming it up isn't nearly the same." I'm flooded with a feeling I can't define—a little bit of my own warmth spreading through me.

Of course, Julie Louise Paris lets herself in. Why wouldn't she? I assume Asher left the door unlocked for her, so she just breezes into the living room. It's seven in the morning on a Monday, and yes, I realize I have about ten minutes to call in sick to work, but if I'm not going to get fired, maybe my boss can help me out with that one. But that would seem like I'm pulling favors because we're supposed to be dating, and pulling favors like that is kind of unfair, so maybe I should get my phone out.

My attention is completely captured by Asher's granny, who is wearing a neon pink sparkly dress, knee-high white boots, and a long black cardigan, also with sequins on the front. It's somehow the most inappropriate, loud outfit yet the most gorgeous thing I've ever seen, all at the same time.

"My goodness, you two look like a pair of somber Tombers this morning," she says, as perky and chipper as if it were three in the afternoon, and she'd just had six espresso shots. Which maybe she has. Who knows. I wouldn't put it past her.

"Sit, Granny, please," Asher grunts. He motions to the spot on the couch, and I take my usual place on the loveseat.

Julie Louise Paris seems to fill up the entire room, and not because the sparkles on her outfit are catching the light from the windows and blinding me but because her personality is just that huge. She looks me over then scans her grandson.

"Ahhh," she says. "I see that someone seems to have found a new residence."

Asher's mouth drops. "Have you been spying on me?"

Julie Louise Paris shrugs. "Absolutely. You didn't think I'd leave everything up to chance, did you? Ha! I suppose you've also figured out that I was paying to provide you with a fake girlfriend."

"I don't know why you did that," Asher says evenly, his voice hard. He seems to take the news of his granny freaking *watching* him and *me* in stride. "Did you not trust that I could take care of it myself?"

"I wanted what was best for you, so I tried to provide it. As I always have. It's complicated, as per usual. Nothing about you or your mom was ever simple, but I guess maybe I'm kind of to blame for that."

"No. You're not. I've made my own decisions, and so has my mom. You've stuck with us through all of it. I love the heck out of you, Granny, so I'm not mad about it because I know that somehow, you must have had my best interests at heart. I'm just sad you had to threaten Emily with losing her job and also swear her to silence."

Julie Louise Paris wrinkles her nose and also raises a brow, which is beyond talented if you ask me. I'm not sure how she does it. "I didn't know you'd actually be interested in her for real. I thought you'd keep a professional level of detachment. She was so different from anyone else that I thought she'd be good for you as a moral compass and also as someone you wouldn't get your wires crossed over."

"Which basically means I was boring and normal, so you thought he wouldn't be interested in a shrew like me."

"Something like that," Julie Louise Paris says cheerfully and openly. Lord, she's more chipper than a wood chipper. See how creative I am first thing in the morning?

"Well, it happened," Asher retorts. "And it caused some serious problems when I found out you'd turned Emily into a double agent."

"Technically, you did that. I got to her first," Julie Louise Paris cackles.

Asher leans back against the couch, totally exasperated. I feel like the conversation is going on around me but not including me at all, and I feel like an outsider looking in. It's not exactly a great feeling when my future with Asher is practically hanging in the balance.

"I think if you like her, you should go for it. Who cares how it started? She would have eventually told you about me, I'm sure. Or I would have confessed when I sensed it was serious. I tried to come between you two, to intervene and make sure I was keeping everyone honest and also to be sure the little shrew wasn't a fortune hunter, but you still called me here this morning even after you found the cheque, so I thought you finally figured it out."

"Hey!" I protest the gold-digging shrew comment.

Asher rolls his eyes and also manages not to look away from his granny. "What's that? What do I have figured out?"

"You finally met someone who made you think, made you want to work things out, and made you want to stay the night even if you were angry and ornery. You didn't want to walk out because you're already attached. I could

Mr. Charming (Not)

tell at dinner, just from how you looked at her, which is exactly what I wanted for you, except none of it can be faked or bought. You found something that is totally, completely real even though Emily knows all about you. She knows you have a name and that you're rich and powerful, but that's not at all why she's with you. She was with you because she had to be, for the money at first, but I can tell that when she looks at you, she doesn't give two flying figs about that. About any of that. She looks at your muscles and nice hair, and she gets lost in your eyes. It's incredibly sappy, and it melts my heart. I gave her the cheque, and I wanted to make sure you saw it because I wanted you to find out. I wanted her to tell you or for you to find out some other way and then have to fight for each other because it's how you know something is real."

"Granny! For the love of—"

"A gorgeous sequin dress that fits like a glove? Yes, I know. It was very meddlesome of me. But an old lady has to meddle, especially in her wonderful, favorite, and only grandson's life—when he needs it. Because, trust me, you need it."

I have to admit I'm about to break out the popcorn. This has been very entertaining, watching Asher and his granny go at it. It's also a little heartbreaking—I mean it in a good way—seeing how much they love each other. Although it was slightly salty to be referred to as a small rodent multiple times and be discussed as though I'm not sitting there, with pronouns being thrown in to stand in place of my actual name, I don't really mind it now.

"So?" Julie Louise Paris asks. "What are you going to do? Are you going to call it quits on what is, in my opinion, one of the best women you've ever had the privilege of going out with, or are you going to realize that affection is complicated, messy, hard, wild, sometimes sketchy, mostly great, a little heartbreaking, often disappointing, though also often not disappointing, and many other words, labels, names, conundrums, and contradictions?"

"You truly are the world's most bizarre grandmother," Asher sighs, but there is real affection in his tone now.

"I know. The one and only. I wouldn't be Julie Louise Paris if I weren't Julie Louise Paris."

Hmm. Apparently, even Julie Louise Paris refers to herself as Julie Louise Paris. Good to know. It's also good to know that in her absolutely crazy sort of way, she's given us her blessing. All of a sudden, she stands up, gives Asher a grin, then sweeps out of the room and out of the house altogether.

I have to say that I'm stunned.

I haven't even had a sip of my coffee, and some serious wisdom already went down in this room. I pick it up now, inhaling the delicious scent of dark, greasy beans. I take a sip and find it still warm. What a treat, although iced coffee is fine by me too. As long as it's the top half. Asher's right. I never drink the bottom bits. There never fails to be tiny grounds in the last bit, and gritty coffee has never been my thing.

"Well?" Asher arches one dark brow as he rifles a hand through his rich brown hair. "What do you have to say to that?"

Here's the advantage of being left out of an entire conversation. At least I had time to observe and think. "I guess she's right, maybe? There was a lot said, and I...I think it would be nice to start over, to give us a chance. I didn't expect it, but I enjoyed our dates. Um, I enjoyed you, and I don't mind you, which is probably the highest praise I've given anyone in a long time. I know my parents love you, and there are still lots of friends and family I want you to meet. Plus, if we gave up now, the media would seriously enjoy that. We'd have been really short-lived. Not that I care what they say because I don't. And you probably don't either. Your granny probably also doesn't now. So that's not really an issue. I'm just saying."

"So you'd like to actually give it a real try? Start afresh? No bad taco dates, no meddling grannies, no opera, no backyard fences on fire, no awkward dinners, no ordering an entire dessert menu, no hacked up tables and brand new ones in pieces, no spontaneous kisses, no—"

"I kind of liked the spontaneous kisses. And the rest. I still have those desserts if you have a craving for extreme amounts of sugar for breakfast."

"You know, I actually do. Cherry pie? Is there any of that?"

"There is, yes. And also blueberry, apple, and chocolate pies."

"Good. That's good," Asher says as he slaps his jean-clad thighs. "Well, if you're good to give this a try, then so am I. I didn't go back to bed last night. I just stayed up and thought. Mostly about you. Well, all about you and about us. About how this past week or so has been the most adventurous one I've ever been on, which is saying a lot because I've been all over the world. Those spontaneous kisses were pretty amazing."

"Please tell me you've also kissed a lot of toads. Does it work for guys that way too?"

"I have," he replied good-naturedly. "And maybe it does. I've also kissed a lot of non-toads, and they still don't hold a candle to you. You're not a princess, you're not a toad, and you're not a shrew."

"Thank god for that," I giggle. Then, more soberly, I

add, "Are you sure you're not still mad about what happened? That you don't doubt me? That you feel like you can trust me?"

"I was mad, but I got over it sometime during the early morning hours. As for trust, it's only been a week, so I think we can give each other the benefit of the doubt because we'll both need to. And as all good shrinks say, work on building each other up, not tearing each other down. The trust will come with time, I'm sure. And like my granny said, I really do want to put that in. The time, I mean. Which is a first for me, so if you feel slightly out to sea, I feel just as out to pasture."

"That's...wow. I...you're right. I was gearing up for one heck of a fight, and I thought I'd truly blown it—the best chance I'd ever been given. Because you're you, and I can see that, even if no one else can. You've *let* me see that, and if your granny says you're already attached, then I'm also already attached."

Asher smiles softly at me, and I take it as an ultra-encouraging sign. I start to relax more and more as the knots begin to work themselves out of my neck, shoulders, and every other tightly wound muscle in my body.

"You're just you, and I really appreciate that," he starts, his voice barely more than a whisper. It's fresher than a pan of buns straight from the oven, and it sends shivers racing up and down my arms. "You're refreshingly honest, crazy with an ax. You're someone who likes fire a little bit too much and someone who can hold her own with fart jokes. I really want to get to know you, Emily. Better than I already do. Much better. I know it was rocky and crazy and bumpy as hell, but from now on, maybe things will calm down. I think about doing all these things in my life, and when I think about doing them without you, they just all feel pretty empty. With some effort, I think we can cut down on the chaos and keep the good parts."

"Like the kisses? Spontaneous and otherwise?"

"Yes."

"Shit!" I jump up, remembering that I've forgotten all about work. Asher's eyes widen. It's clearly not the reaction he was expecting. "Work!" I clarify. "I should call in..."

"Me too."

"But if we both do, won't it look extremely suspicious?"

"Who cares?" Asher grins at me. "I'm the boss. And dating the boss has a whole set of perks. You call, then I'll call. And after that, we can talk more about desserts and kisses."

Even though he just told me to call, Asher walks over, wraps his arms around my waist, and gives me one of those delicious, wonderful, spur-of-the-moment kisses we were just discussing. I melt like melty melted butter in his arms, and there's no way I'm not grateful for another chance. The road has indeed been rocky, mountainous, treacherous, icy, windblown, washed out, full of holes and pitfalls, and everything else it can be, but we're still on it. Or maybe we've just veered off onto a different one—one that's ours, of our own choosing and making.

I'm seriously glad. I pour everything I have into the kiss, and when Asher finally pulls back, I treat him to a dose of his own medicine. I smile, I shrug, and then I crook a finger, beckoning him into the kitchen for breakfast. The first one of many we'll share together. How fitting that I have an entire fridge of tasty treats to choose from. But even without that, though, I know I'd never forget it.

EPILOGUE
EMILY

*J*ulie Louise Paris did indeed take her last name from the city. Currently, it's where I live. Paris. I think it's legit one of the most beautiful places on earth. And no. It's not at all dirty. I really can't believe I once said that. Oh, and my last name? It's also now Paris. Yet another reason to like the city.

"Coffee?"

"Argh!" I nearly jumped straight out of the window seat I've been curled up in for the last half hour, an unread book on my lap.

Asher grins apologetically at me. "Sorry, I didn't mean to scare you." He's wearing a red and blue plaid jacket and jeans. I take in the jacket, and now I'm the one grinning.

"Supporting your granny's new clothing line, I see."

"Don't," he threatens mockingly. "Just don't."

It's different, that's for sure, because it's the first time I've ever seen Asher wear anything like it. My husband is the most gorgeous man in the world, at least to me, so it looks beyond stellar on him, but I'm not entirely sure about Julie Louise Paris' new line. Yes, she's still designing.

Mr. Charming (Not)

She says the last designs she'll ever make are the ones she's buried in, so she has no plans to quit anytime soon.

I smooth a hand over my rounded belly and accept the coffee. I sip it, and it's not great since it's decaf, but I can handle it for another few months. At seven months pregnant, I'm already more than ready to meet our daughter. I've had a healthy pregnancy, but it started with me being incredibly sick. That lasted for about four months, and now I'm just nauseated, like one hundred percent of the time. I can't imagine how anyone bears children because I still haven't gotten to the part where my belly is so big that I topple over or feel like I'm being crushed. And then there's the birth to look forward to. Which I'm really not looking forward to. Obviously.

"I won't," I say, holding in a giggle. "It looks good on you. I'm just not sure about the rest of the world."

Asher's eyes shine like the Paris sky outside the window. "Thank you. I'm sure Granny knows what she's doing. She always seems to pull everything off."

"If there's anyone who can do it, she can."

"You look ravishing this morning," he murmurs, eyeing me.

I stand slowly and massage the kinks out of my shoulders. "Do I?" I'm still in my fluffy purple cat housecoat. I haven't given it up because I love it.

"Do you know what purple puffiness does for me?"

I walk over to the coffee table in the expansive living room and set my coffee cup down. "No. Why don't you tell me?"

"You're the woman I love, and you'd look good in anything but the best in nothing. That sounds like a riddle."

I snort as Asher closes the distance and wraps his arms

around my waist. He leans in, which despite the massive bump between us, is still easy for him because he's so tall. With a small satisfied sigh, I rest my hands on his shoulders and savor his kiss.

"I love you too. And I think that riddle also applies to you."

People call us a rags to riches story. Okay, they call me that since I married Asher Paris, the billionaire. Then, I moved to Paris. I have this huge house, all the money in the world, and a thriving business we own. But most of all, I have the world's actual best man as my partner. I personally think it's slightly rude to call it rags to riches because, I mean, I never wore rags. I wore nice fair trade clothing from the company we still own, thank you very much. And the money, fame, and allure of Paris...none of it could have made up my mind. It was all Asher. From that first kiss on the sidewalk.

"Did your mom get back to you yet? About when they're coming?"

"Next week, actually. We better have the guest room ready."

My parents are going to come for a few months and help us after the baby is born. I know we could hire anyone, but no one is my mom. And I'd also like to see my dad. We still spend a lot of time in the States, and we make sure we visit my parents and my brothers' families as often as we can, but still.

Asher's mom and granny actually live close by, so we'll have lots of support when our daughter arrives.

"Names," Asher says seriously as he kisses me on the corner of the mouth again. "We better think of some because people have been asking me for months."

"Yup. Since we made the announcement."

Mr. Charming (Not)

"I guess that's what we get for creating the world's most adorable baby."

"You haven't even seen her yet!"

"I know. But I know she'll look like you, so she'll be beautiful in every way."

"Oh geez." I punch Asher on the shoulder playfully. "You're going to help your granny today?"

"I am." Asher works all around with his granny since he's taken a more active role as head of the company.

"Okay, have fun."

"You know I will. We're getting ready to launch the new line, so Granny's in a fit and flurry."

"When is she not?"

"You're right." Asher kisses me on the mouth again. "She always is."

"She has more energy than anyone I know."

"She does. I sometimes feel like she could run a marathon if it's what she decided to do. With zero training to boot. She'd just jump right in and probably still outrun everyone."

I laugh. "God, she's excited to be a great granny." She wants us to name our daughter Monica after her own mother, and I like the name. I actually like it a lot.

"She is. And though my mom is less than excited to have the term grandmother, she's still overjoyed to be one."

Asher's mom might have been wild back in the day, but she's really settled down. She now lives in Paris full time and has been helping in the company. She's loved me from the first, and she was overjoyed to hear we were going to have a baby. She said she wanted it to be a girl, though a boy would also have been acceptable and equally loved. Her exact words. Her smile was so big when she found out the baby was really a girl.

I give Asher two more kisses before pulling away. It's weird for me not to be working on something or other, like some marketing or going over details with Asher. He's been trying to ease me off of it since he doesn't want me to get stressed out, but also because I want to be a full-time mom after I give birth. It's getting closer and closer, so even I've been trying to cut back on work duties.

"Wait. Forgot one for the road." Asher bends and gives me another kiss.

I know he's already late, so I watch him stalk around the house, gathering up his wallet and keys, and wave as he goes out the door. He'll be back in a few hours, and I'm bound and freaking determined to get the nursery set up. I've bought wallpaper and paint, the furniture, rugs, lamps, and it's all just kind of sitting around waiting for us to get to it.

Maybe I'll roll up my sleeves this morning, drink my decaf, and start on the painting. It's non-toxic, safe paint, and I bought some wallpaper too. I figure it might end up a disaster, but I'm still going to try. No matter how the nursery turns out, it's going to be perfect because it's going to be yet another thing we create together.

It's been three years and seven months since I kissed him outside my workplace, and I think we've made a pretty great team over the years. We got married two years ago and then made Paris our permanent residence after the wedding. We got married in Paris, and I'll never forget how wonderful that day was. I'll never forget any day I've spent with Asher because they've all been wonderful.

And I know for a fact that we'll have plenty more where those came from, days filled with smiles and shrugs.

The End.

ALPHALICIOUS BILLIONAIRES BOX SET 3

Ever met the exquisitely hot boss from hell? No?

Well, meet Curtis James, jerk of the century, owner of the most perfect jawline with a gift for rapping instructions faster than a seasoned rapper.

And guess what, he is actually asking for my help for once... to babysit kids!

I am not going to lie, I nearly died of shock.

SNEAK PEAK OF THE BOX SET

Lexi

Everyone had their price. It turned out that Lexi Wellington's was ten thousand. Ten thousand dollars for two days of babysitting wasn't bad. It worked out to a little over two hundred and eight dollars an hour. Well over the thirty-two dollars an hour she was making as a receptionist to the biggest jerk in Seattle.

Curtis James wasn't just Seattle's most eligible bachelor.

He was the head of a multi-billion-dollar corporation that made and sold kitchen implements of all things. She'd grown up with the James name in her household. Actually, three generations had because that's how old the company was. Broderick James started the whole thing with a hundred-dollar loan and his incredible ingenuity in his garage after his wife complained about her hand-held cake mixer. Patrick James continued his father's legacy, expanding at an incredible rate, mass producing, and taking the company global. Curtis James got to inherit the whole dang empire when his father retired.

Just like most entitled, trust-fund brats, Curtis James did absolutely nothing with his life. His friends called him Curt, but Lexi wasn't one of his friends. She used to call him, at least in her mind, The Big D, which stood for The Big Douchebag, but then she finally realized what else it could stand for- and she certainly DID NOT know anything about him having a big D- she knocked that right off. She settled instead for TFB, Trust Fund Baby, only in her head of course. It was apt, seeing as he rarely showed up at the office and on days that he did, it was to bark orders in meetings and shit all over everyone's happiness and no- he didn't shit rainbows and glitter. More the real, gross, nasty kind of shit that no one ever wanted to smell, step in, deal with, or clean up.

Most of the time she didn't mind her job. It was those rare moments, the ten percent of the time, when she actually had to deal with the TFB, that she would rather stick a fork in her eye repeatedly and viciously, than show up to work.

How she let James talk her into her current predicament was beyond her. Oh right. He actually used the word *please*, probably for the first time in his spoiled, shallow existence, and sweetened the pot with ten thousand dollars- after taxes- if she was willing to show up at his house at seven on a Friday night and stay until four on Sunday.

And no. None of James' anatomy was involved in the bargain. She might be his executive assistant. She might have sandy blonde hair and be okay in the looks department as far as she was concerned. She might even wear the occasional pencil skirt and pair it with high heels because she liked to show up to work looking at least semi-professional, but no. She wasn't a cliché. She wasn't going to her boss' house to gamble on her career. She was there to do what The TFB viewed as the impossible: babysit his niece and nephew for the weekend.

Unfortunately, Curtis James would be there as well. Duh. They were his sister's kids and for some crazy reason- which he hadn't fully explained when he called her into his office mid-week to ask her to save his sorry non-rainbow shitting hide- he'd agreed to look after them for the weekend. He'd debriefed her quick. Given her his usual to the point, asshole list, rattled off like he was reading from some actual bullet pointed paper he'd committed to memory.

Curtis hated kids. He also made it clear he would never have kids of his own. But he had a sister and apparently, she didn't hate kids. And unfortunately for him, she'd decided to go and have her own kids. And now, she and her husband wanted to go away for the weekend. When Lexi asked why he'd agreed just like that to be the "sacrificial lamb" here, the TFB said that his sister actually begged, pleaded and even produced actual tears until he agreed to look after her kids. And that she didn't trust a babysitter.

He also emphasized to her several times over how

much he actually loathed children. Especially the four and two year old variety. He was in deep shit (that was implied, he didn't actually say it). Would she be willing to help him for the weekend?

And Lexi wasn't like Curtis James at all. She actually loved kids. At twenty-seven, she wasn't exactly ready for her own yet, but she was actually pretty okay with babysitting not that she had had much chance to do that for the past couple of years. Her brother and sister, both younger, also weren't ready for settling down and starting families and most of her friends were either single or just getting into that committed stage and didn't have kids either. But she had done her fair share of babysitting when she was in high school, so she had some experience and was more than ready.

Curtis James- she usually thought of him in the formal sense and not just because he was her boss, but because he was douchy and spoiled enough to deserve it- didn't know her at all. If he'd have asked her if she could pull some overtime in the form of babysitting and offered to pay her normal wage plus overtime, she would have actually agreed. She loved kids that much.

Okay... so maybe there was a little other motivation involved. Maybe she thought Curtis James was hot. So what? He was easy on the eyes. That was just her unfortunate biology acting up. Damn ovaries. She couldn't help that the guy was walking sex. Lickable to a fault. Even if he was an asshole with a side helping of unwiped asshole assholeness, she still had eyes. And he was still delicious. Maybe that played a small part in her final decision. Maybe. Like, one percent of the motivation. At least twenty percent was the money and the other seventy-nine was the kids.

Long story short, it was how she wound up in front of James' sprawling mansion, out of breath, flustered from getting stuck in traffic, trying to smooth out the wrinkles in her skirt and shoulder her duffel bag at the same time. She knocked once. Just a light rap, but it was enough. The door slowly creaked open in front of her. The thing was huge, like fourteen feet high kind of huge. It was a double wood structure that was probably made on the other side of the world and cost a hundred grand alone. It wasn't carved or anything, past the usual detailing that everyone else had on their normal sized doors, but she knew James' arrogance would stop at nothing. He probably had to have a fourteen-foot double door because no one else in the ridiculously ritzy, gated community of mansions and billionaires had one.

She actually expected a butler. Ok, maybe more like a housekeeper.

She nearly died of shock.

There was no butler or maid. Nope. That hugely overcompensated door creaked open and there was the TFB himself.

In jeans and a t-shirt. Looking extremely uncomfortable. Out of his element. Strangely vulnerable. Sinfully, mouth-wateringly, deliciously, ultra-eye pleasing. He was the tastiest of eye candy. Instead of standing there and taking in his full six foot something, bronzed skin, muscles galore, too tight t-shirt clad chest, veiny popping forearms, wicked jeans, tousled mahogany hair, face carved out of diamonds and the tears of angels, Lexi cleared her throat, pursed her lips, raised a brow, and slammed on her best no-nonsense face.

Oh yeah. She was not currently burning up on the spot. Her ovaries were definitely not hurting either. Nope.

Turning into a furnace, internally or otherwise, after a blast of the TFB's hotness wasn't on the menu for her weekend.

"I'm here," she whisper-yelped. Her voice was all wrong. Too dry. Too thin. Choked up. Of course, the bastard would do something as stupid as not wear a suit in his own house. How freaking dare he be allowed to look like a normal person once in a while? She cleared her throat and tried again. "So? I'm here. Where are the kids?"

"The monsters you mean?" James' ultra-delicious, ultra-jerk lips thinned out. "Inside. Tearing my house apart."

"You left them unattended?"

"Only for a minute so I could answer the damn door." Curtis James stepped out, towering over her, all delicious muscly goodness. He smelled different than he did when he walked into the office, boasting something strong even though it was a scent-free zone. He smelled less like stinky pines and more like unhinged, stressed, sweaty masculinity and sharp aftershave. In essence, he was manly and mysterious and that made Lexi's legs feel a little watery. Her internal furnace kicked up a few nonsense notches.

Just then, from out of nowhere, a dark haired, cherub faced blur streaked by the gigantic open door. "Uncle!" The little girl wailed, blue eyes wide, little bow lips quivering, her delicate cheeks stained pink. "Austin got his diaper off and he smeared poop all over the wall!"

While Curtis James' face drained of blood and his glacier blue eyes rolled in their sockets, Lexi stepped in, grinning wide. It was funny how a toddler and a bit of poo could take even Seattle's most eligible douchwad down a couple of notches. *Take that, TFB.* There was the possibility that this weekend might just, unexpectedly, be the best of her life.

The Alphalicious Billionaires Box Set is now available on Amazon.

ABOUT THE AUTHOR

Lindsey Hart specializes in sweet to extra hot and dirty romances and strongly believes in happily ever after. If you are looking for a page turner, then you are in for a wild and naughty ride with feisty heroines and alpha male heroes.

Made in the USA
Monee, IL
23 November 2022